The Stories of James

James - brother of Jeshua, (Jesus)
~ the Sun of Love ~

James Francis

Copyright © James Francis, 2022
Published: 2022 by The Book Reality Experience

ISBN: 978-1-922670-49-6 - Paperback Edition
ISBN: 978-1-922670-50-2 – E-Book Edition

All rights reserved.

The right of James Francis to be identified as the author of this Work has been asserted by him in accordance with sections 77 and 78 of the Copyright, Designs and Patents Act 1988.

The information contained in this book is the author's own thoughts and interpretations of religious texts. They represent the author's faith and interpretations and should not be construed as being representative of the publisher.

Any resemblance to actual persons, living or dead, is purely coincidental.

No part of this publication may be reproduced, stored in a retrieval system, copied in any form or by any means, electronic, mechanical, photocopying, recording or otherwise transmitted without written permission from the publisher.
You must not circulate this book in any format.

Cover Design by Luke Buxton | www.lukebuxton.com

Dedication:

To Gaby, Brent and LeeAnne, Ben and Maureen, Savannah, my Brothers and Sisters, Paul and Violet, Greg, Mick, Tim, Ann, Mary, Carole and Bill, Duncan, and their children and grandchildren, and Jefferson. James and Joshua. Bret and Tammy, Billy and Kelly and their beloved families.

    Friends, Peggy and Greg, Sharon, Tammy and Carrie, Logan, Hannah, Farley, Jeremy, Paul, Linda and Dave, Stephanie and Sapphire, Dave and Nichole, Buddy, Doug, Danae, Sierra, Vern, Roger and Breezy. Old friends, Dennis, Dan, Gary, Bud and Julie, and Denise. Gracie, Angie, Malcolm and Diane. Dave and Pam, and sweet friend Rhonda. Chris and Kate, Josh and Andra and Jeremy. And those that have passed, Grandma and Grandpa, Mom and Dad, Fred and Mary, Rob and Faye, Tim, Bob, Marcel, and Maxine, and Leanne. And once again, to my Beloved Kaye, until we reunite, all my love,

James
2022

Dedication: i

Introduction v

~The Veil~ 1

~ His Gift of Speech and Conversation ~ 3

~ "Blasphemer" cries the Temple priest ~ 5

~ Visitors of Holy Fire ~My mother, Mariam or ~Mary~ 12

~ Josephs Visions, the Wondrous Carpentry of Life ~ 14

~ My Cup Runneth Over ~ 18

~ As a Boy, Jeshua Heals a Sparrow~ 21

~ Human Laughter, to ride the Breath of Joy ~ 23

~Joy and Work~ 25

~ A Mother's Love~ 27

~ Jeshua interprets our cousin John's Dream, ... 29

~ Master Gardner, True Servant of the Most High ~ 32

~Being True to the Spiritual Self, above Earthly concerns ~ 35

~ Simon and Andrew, the Kind Fishermen ~ 39

~My Brother Jude~ 42

~Born Captains of God, Sailing the Sea of Love~ 44

~Father, Your Work is Well Accomplished~ 46

~John the Baptizer and the Blind Man's Vision~ 49

~Jeshua Returns~ 58

~Jeshua Baptized~ 60

~Evil never truly was, except as a Compass for the Soul ~ 63

~The Blind Man~ 66

~The Adulteress~ 68

~ Every Man is the Temple of God, and His Soul, the Portal of Divinity ~ 70

~ My Kingdom is not of this World ~ 75

~ After the time of my Mission being Complete ~ 80

~The Crippled Child~ 82

~The Kingdom of The Father~ 84

~Our Father's Purposes and Will~ 88

~The Gift of a Woman~ 89

~The Olive Fields~ 91

~The Fields of Forgiveness~ 94

~The Sorrows of Man~ 96

~The Heart, So Saith Jeshua~ 98

~ After the Last Supper ~ 100

~Jeshua Appears to me Among The Olive Trees~ 103

~ Shalom said the Roman Visitor~ 106

~Be Not Afraid, It is I.~ Resurrection-A Golden Sunset~ 109

About the Author 113

Acknowledgements 115

Introduction

This discourse is not given to represent a history of biblical events, so much as it is offered as reflections and testimonies of redemption and resurrection, for such is the destiny of the Soul.

~ For There Came the Love of Eternal Divine Forces from the Pastures of the Brilliant One, that being our Father-Mother and Creator, who would visit His Heart before and upon all men thru the Life and Light of this Son. This Masterful Soul and Our Brother in Spirit being Holy Anointed as the Path Maker of Our Great Brotherhood of Souls, bears True Witness and Companionship with Our Father and His Creative Purposes, Essence of Will and Love thereof ~

He walked among us so that Man could hear, see and know of the Great Truth of His Own Heritage. Jesus taught that one should earnestly seek and pray to know the Will of Our Father's Spirit within and awaken the Kingdom of God. You embody within your soul the Eternal Spark of the Father, the Priceless Pearl of your Divine Nature. This is the Living Truth of Every Man and Entity Incarnate upon the Material Journey. Throughout the all and unending

Heavenly Kingdoms and Spiritual Domains of the Soul, as well as here in physical realms, we are called to remember that we are the Sons of Our Father's Love and Our Destiny is wholly assured and perfected in Him as Companions of the Infinite Expression of Creative Forces within all Life.

We are the Immortal and Blessed Sons and Daughters of God, and the Great Revelation of this Truth was then manifested within the experience of Man thru the Material bestowal of the Life of Jesus, our Elder Brother being both a man and yet One married in complete oneness to the Will of the Divine Forces of the Fathering Spirit of Creation, or God. And He handed us the keys to the Kingdom of Our Father as He taught, "Love the Father with all your heart and soul, and your brother and neighbor as being that same Self, just as I have loved you."

The Whispering Voice of Compassion, Love and Mercy, that beats upon the doors of Man's Heart is the Language of the Soul. If you would know the Heart of your Father then Seek to know your Own for they are One and the Same. The Graciousness of This Attending Presence and Perfect Intention lives always within your journey. Loving one another respects our Truth and gives Honor to All Life and the One Source.

Chapter 1

~The Veil~

I was born James, and first brother to Jeshua ~ Jesus ~ who had come into this world nearly four years prior. And so it was that I followed Him, like so many of us who have followed with Him from our earliest beginnings of this glorious Journey of Spirit in Soul and Body.

The Veil drops and I awaken as a hungry child under a blazing sun. Then, warmly bathed, I am gently tucked and folded in a blanket and lamb skin. I sleep and am well nurtured as a babe. Several years pass till I am found to be a crab-walking toddler in a dusty gathering of knees and noise. I feel protected yet unsafe. The sound of the voices in this gathering place of men, animals, coins, and soldiers, makes my skin burn with tension, and I wish not to have my hand let go of. But it falls free and I fear I will be lost when suddenly a new hand takes mine and I am instantly steadied.

I see Him, the background of the sun behind Him making His dark brown curls shine like red and gold grapes. He smiles and I see and feel an assured safety in His eyes and from His hand, a safety not felt in the hands of others.

As a very young man, I loved Him. He was my older brother and my friend. But I also feared for Him, and for myself as well, for He was a Pure Lamb from God sent into a world filled with the dens of wolves. Within me grew an awareness, a feeling of being locked into oncoming events. On the day of my twelfth birthday, He told me of certain visions He had seen about the future and He said, **"Do not be alarmed James, that I should so soon prepare you. Just as those events of divine markings have preceded us, so also now comes the Rain of the Father's Love and Will to live among us, in these, the long awaited and appointed Times."** I was much alarmed. Though I always found His words convincing and received them deep within me, knowing that He must be One of the Chosen Ones who are taken from within by The Great Spirit of Truth and Life, yet I did not want to believe Him. I did not want to believe in parts of His visions that spoke of mayhem and crucifixion, and even of a resurrection. Often I wrestled with fear and anguish for thoroughly and without pause I believed every word that ever fell from His lips, even when I did not fully understand Him. It would require a lifetime of experience for me to more fully comprehend the Truth of His words and the purposes of His mission. This also I would tell you now and with sincere declaration; though I let go of His hand more than a few times, He never let go of mine and He held that same great love for everyone.

Chapter 2

~ His Gift of Speech and Conversation ~

Jeshua was remarkably gifted in speech and conversation. From His earliest interactions as a child, it was noticed readily by everyone around Him that His words were always pointedly delivered and He seemed never to waste a word. He also bore an immensely inquisitive nature, which was relentlessly employed in His search for the understanding of the nature of all the things of heaven and earth and of the ways and affairs of men. His questions contained their answer, and His answers and replies made you question your thoughts and look within before speaking.

He shunned arguments and ended them by getting right to the heart of the matter in His discourse. And greatest of all was the humbling, comforting, inspiring, illuminating healing eloquence of His teaching manner. Whether engaging in personal encounters or teaching among throngs of listeners, His Presence, Voice, Authority, and Love was Magnetic, feel-able, and compelled great attention from every association that He entered into.

His questions and answers brought alarm and conflict to those brothers who would position themselves as opponents, for they provided a sudden, and sometimes unwelcome, injection of Truth into these discussions. Jeshua's words and voice pierced in such a way that all who heard Him were jarred into reflecting on their own thoughts; one would suddenly know where one's darkness and error lay.

The revelation of such nakedness within was not always well received, especially among those who felt they had much to hide from themselves and others. Jeshua took no joy in overcoming those who sought to entrap or outwit Him but He never wavered in His delivery of Truth. Those priests and men who sought to show Him up as inferior found themselves inwardly disturbed, for as He said, **"Many have in error built their temples of peace and comfort out of the mere twine and threads of their very thin robes."** The air would fill with their frustrated gasps as though a great insult had taken their breath from them for their religious thrones hung precariously upon the illusion and pious assumption that they held a holy rank before God and above other men. To their great dismay, their spiritual shortcomings were often exposed before the common people.

Many of the people became enamored of Him, His compassion, words, and His healing touch, and did not welcome rude intrusions pressed upon their brother and teacher. Often Jeshua's enemies became enraged, some dangerously so.

Chapter 3

~ "Blasphemer" cries the Temple priest ~

I was present when Jeshua taught and ministered outside the walls of Jerusalem to a crowd of poor and hungry-for-hope souls. A child stood with Him, Jeshua's hand resting lovingly upon his head. Suddenly my brother was set upon by a group of menacing and already agitated temple priests, who arrogantly pushed their way into His midst and demanded his attention. Jeshua turned and said to them, **"What is it that you seek, you the keepers of the Law and Word? Have you come to bring food for the hungry and peace to the weary? Or do your real intentions lie robed and hidden behind this impious demonstration of your stature before men?"** There was a hush among those gathered. The most sumptuously robed priest spoke gruffly saying "We have come to see and hear for ourselves the Nazarene who speaks of the Lord saying the Kingdom of God is at hand. Are you then who we seek?" Jeshua replied, **"It is well for you to seek after me for freely I bring you the Truth of your Heavenly Father. But you men whose understanding of your Heavenly Creator is locked away in the dense cloud of this world can neither see nor hear nor** truly know me or the Divine Lord of Life who has sent me, for your vision is blurred, your ears are deaf and your minds and hearts are soiled and in darkness."

The disturbance those words created was obvious, not only upon the faces of the priests but in their gasps of displeasure. Their angry grumblings hissed like a venomous snake that wound its tail around their spokesman and leader who angrily challenged Jeshua again saying, "Nazarene, why do you insult us? You say we cannot see you, yet are you not plainly in our sight? Through what devil do you say this to us? Have you not preached unto our people saying the Kingdom of God is at hand?" Jeshua looked away from the priest and down onto the child who held his garment and said, **"Behold the child who resides even now within the Kingdom of God. His Heart is Pure, Innocent of Judgment, and he thinks not that he is better than another. And though still hungry, he offered me the share of his bread. I tell you even now he is full with the Kingdom of God, and so yes, even closer than his hand is the Kingdom of God within him. And until you become as pure as this child you will never see that His Kingdom is already within you."**

Jeshua then looked up at the priests and said, **"Are not the only devils speaking here those that hide in fear of losing their stature and their wealth? Who among you has accepted the offerings of these your poor but without humbleness and gratitude for God's abundance set upon your table? Look now into the garden of your thoughts and pull the weeds of your own making. Make yourself clean of heart and mind if you would enter the Kingdom of the Lord. Embrace the Spirit of Love within each day, even each hour of the life awarded you. It is written, "The Lord thy God is One and the Heavens and Earth are the Handiwork of His**

Presence." You cannot love and serve God without also loving your brother as yourself. We are of One Brotherhood by the very Breath of Our Father, none being greater or lesser than the next. Those that hear my words are already saved, while those that fear my words know only of the earth, and even of that but little, and nothing of the Heavenly Kingdoms."

The voice of another priest then shouted from behind the group, "By what authority say you these things to us? Do you claim to know the mind of God and His workings better than us? Are you then a prophet proclaiming yourself before the people? Tell us Nazarene, do you then claim to carry the words of God? Answer well, for perilous is the road of the blasphemer."

Jeshua answered with great force upon his lips, like arrows cast from a Quiver of Truth. **"I shall not answer by my own authority, but by the Father who hath sent me. He has placed His Words upon my tongue, His Light within my Heart, and His Will upon my mind."** Speaking to both the people and the temple priests he said, **"Heed then the Will of the Holy One. Love thy neighbor as your friend and brother, for Every Man is the Temple of God whose Spirit you awaken even as you give thanks unto the sun and rain, the birds in the air and all creatures upon the earth and within its waters. Rejoice when toiling in the fields that bring plants to bear you their fruit and grains, and for the seas that fill your plates with fish. So also does the earth offer up her soil, stone and wood as bricks and wall for shelter. See how the wool of His sheep has clothed you and kept you warm in the cold of night. In all things has God provided for the needs of the body, so that the Spirit and Soul of Man could partake of the Material life, this being but just one of the manifold mansions within His Wondrous and Eternal Kingdom.**

Also understand that freely have you chosen this life, those past and even into the future, so that each Soul may complete its purposes and its destiny be then fulfilled. Then shall his soul be resurrected into the Garden of the Holy Place, as the Perfected Seed of the Father."

Then turning his head away from the priests, he said to the people, "Do not despise those who are your leaders and rulers as they also learn from their roles, the lessons of the soul. Do not envy the rich or powerful, for even when their coffers overflow, they live in fear that tomorrow there may be less. So must they learn that he who gains in worldly riches has not found peace within his soul for until the time comes of his greater understanding he is imprisoned in his greed by the tentacles of fear.

So is it also with those kings and rulers of lands and peoples who would make slaves of another people, and even their own. See how they suffer the demons of their own making by fearing their thrones and lands may be taken from them. Their stature and wealth, like all things temporary, are but an illusion; an empty well and hollow tomb. The rise and fall of flesh and earth are the gifts of Perfect Love as provided to the journeying soul by the Father of Stars and Lights. There is nothing to own yet everything to enjoy.

Also seek not to bring harm to any man even though you are justly angered. If he taunts and offends you, strike him not down. Forgive him his trespasses and pray for those who seek to do harm for they know not what they do. They drown in the waters of their fears, and would seek to press others beneath the waves that they may rise above all others.

See how the darkness of their mind is like a net, old and worn, weakened with holes and provides no sanctuary.

There is no peace to be found in men who would reach for the sword to stave off the tide of their fears, or to gain for themselves the life and property of another.

If a robber would demand your shoes, by the Spirit of Love, offer him also your cloak. Let this be without reproach, for in the night when alone with his thoughts he will feel the warmth of your garb and consider the kindness of your gesture. Then, step upon step, he will come to see and feel the warmth of a pure and tender Light upon the horizon, and find it also within his own Temple. So also may he find the Light within him to be that of the Father's Presence and know it to be as great as that of any man or angel. Do not judge the smallest of kindnesses to have no weight, for the ripple of Love is without end and, divinely so Designed, lives in the True Nature of your Father."

"Blasphemer," the voice of another priest cried out. Without pause Jeshua turned to the priest and replied saying, **"To you who now cries blasphemer. It is written upon the Record of your Soul that you were once unfairly and brutally judged, and you found no forgiveness for your transgressors. You created a dark pit that has imprisoned you. So you are now the aggressor. You tread the very path that you so despised. Their pitfalls are now yours. Behold how easy it is to become as they are. But the Lord saith to you, "This day my Son I have forgiven you, and for all your days are you already forgiven." But the hour of your choice is now upon you. Shall it be you who now unfairly judges another and inflicts harm upon the innocent? Do as you will, but neither blind cruelty nor darkened hearts can lessen the Great and Holy Love of the Father for His Children. For when the Son of God is raised upon a hill, you shall see that His arms are outstretched for All man, and though his limbs be broken,**

and body torn and pierced, even then shall be heard the Spirit of Forgiveness upon His lips.

All shall come to know the sweet Grace of the Creator, for He has Written His Light into the Structure of All Life. Within the numberless temples He does abide. Truly I tell you that it is the Will of the Father that Not One of you, the Sons and Daughters of God, can perish from the Gardens of His Love."

The priest who had just cried out in judgment was speechless. His tongue was frozen and his breath stripped from him, for the words of Jeshua had resounded in him like thunder. He was near fainting and pleaded for the support of those beside him. In my nervousness I almost laughed at the spectacle, but bore down hard on myself so that I would not do so, for that would have instantly been seen as mockery and the waters of anger were already stirred. I knew that this was yet another moment on the wheel of events from which there seemed no offer of escape. Any promise of an alternate outcome found secretly dangling in the shadows of this path, felt unlikely. Gradually, I came to understand that there were no shadows where Jeshua stepped, for He carried none within him.

Jeshua turned and walked away from the priests having said what was necessary. The priests, however, were besieged by a swirling inner sense of threat that rattled their foundations, and quite predictably, the demons of their fearful thoughts would harden their hearts further. The High Priest said in quiet anger to his attendants, "We withdraw from this place. Follow me to the temple and speak not of this to anyone, nor between yourselves." But I knew they would soon speak many words among themselves once behind the safety of their walls. They would twist and turn their minds into dark corners to defend their honor. The High Priest would make great and loud supplications to the Lord, like a great peacock who spreads his feathers in a show of authority and righteousness, while disguising the ungodly spirit of contempt and self-flattery that lay within him.

The priests would plot a course that would bring my brother to the Cross he spoke of. It was impossible to protect him. It was always that way. He never retreated from the danger He posed to Himself by angering the temple priests. He could never be silent when everything within him demanded He teach. He had always been uninterested in using his power with the people to ascend an "earthly throne". I and my family were fearful of the outcome of His mission. The anxiety within me grew.

Chapter 4

~ Visitors of Holy Fire ~

My mother, Mariam or ~Mary~

Mary was a Woman befriended by Angels. She quickly grew to know her part in the celestial events that engulfed her soul. Mary became aware of her service to her Heavenly Father thru the Inception of Divine Forces within her womb; The Conception of The Body Temple for the Coming Sun of Love, that would be her son.

Mary was visited several times by Those Messengers that shone Brighter than day. They brought her strength, peace, and word of **"Great tidings for the children of men, for the Promised One is soon delivered into your arms, this Star of Love and Son of God, Whose Light will not be diminished by the shadows and substances of the planes of earth and matter. And Man shall see the Resurrection of His Spirit and Truth upon the Tree of Life, and the Door shall be Opened for All who would follow,"** as was proclaimed by one such Visitor of Holy Fire, who had appeared before the Chosen virgin.

She was a Pearl, a perfect blending of Spirit and Earthly womanhood, betrothed of God and man. As a child, I would follow while she would gather sticks and branches for fire of which I could hold but a few in my small hands. She was also full with child during that time. But what I remember most fondly was the watchfulness of her eyes. Thru them I would come to know of love as persistent, tender, sturdy, protective, and warm. It was my mother's knowing-love that I found to be my refuge for I trusted her above all others. The look of her eyes into mine, even if but a glance, captured my attention every time, and I would find her thought to be immediately planted within me. If then she spoke, the confirmation of her words proceeded forth like a tenderly charming echo.

Chapter 5

~ Josephs Visions, the Wondrous Carpentry of Life ~

Jesoef, or Joseph

My father was esteemed by his brethren and beloved by his family. He was learned in the scriptural doctrines and their history and prophecies. He kept his knowledge as a pearl within rather than parade it before men. He was sincere, strong, upright, humble, and a respecter of all persons. He had become expertly skilled in the working of wood, stone and metals. He showed me from the beginning those methods he applied to the hurdles presented. I was amazed by his talent, though it was not to come quite as easily to me as it had to my older brother. Jeshua now worked by his side while I attended to the needs of the family as instructed by my mother. But my father's patience was deep and I would eventually learn these skills well enough to assist him in his undertakings and services in our home, and in the city and villages of the land as well. And from there, I became proficient enough to meet most of the needs of my family after my father died.

Often he teased me gently in my frustration. One day, as I failed at my task, the following words captured my deep attention. "My son, it could be well for you to be a fisherman, and not the carpenter, lest the house fall down upon us all." He smiled, amused at his jest, while his eyes showed full with tender compassion. In earnest I replied, "But Father, I would honor your footsteps and bring pride unto your namesake." And my father took both my hands and clasped them together, saying, "Then pray often, with your hands like this before your heart, that you only be the hands and workings of your Heavenly Father, and know that my gladness in you is already full and shall be with you in all my days.

You are of the age now to understand more of the things of heaven and earth and the wondrous carpentry of all Life, formed by the Perfect Hands of the Maker. I shall tell you of the following vision that long ago came upon my soul as I slept. This vision came in my seventeenth year, a young man, newlywed and my wife found full with my child."

The ~ Vision ~

"I was in a dark and treacherous storm. Desperately, I searched to find and protect my family for I was filled with trepidation. Then did I see her, my wife heavy with child, tossed upon the seas, soon to drown for I could not reach her. Though I swam swiftly, she drifted further from me and disappeared beneath the waves. I cried out to the Lord that they not be forsaken, and suddenly the storm was no more. I then beheld a blue sky that held bright stars like diamonds and the Voice of the Heavens spoke loudly saying, **"Fear not, for they are in My keeping and shall find repose in the Firmaments of Paradise and be forever sustained."** And I saw many stars that moved from their stations and across the skies they came. The first one was large like the Sun, and of it the Great Voice said, **"This is

my First Born and shall be as King of the Heavens and Earth." Then I saw the other stars following behind the Great Sun and they formed the likeness of a crown, and of these the Lord said, **"Behold the stars of His Crown. By thy seed and others come these fishers of men."** | I awoke from the vision and sat straight up and was glad to see that my wife, now full with child, lay safe asleep beside me. But I was distraught remembering their falling beneath the waters and I circled her in my arm and loved her quietly. And in three days after that vision, truly did I face such a bitter storm for she died in childbirth and my child as well. I cried out her name in great anguish, imploring my Father to bring them into His Eternal Garden and sustain them at the Table of His Peace and Perfect Love.

For many years I did not understand the vision, until I was chosen to be betrothed to your mother. And in that time I was given to know **"That a Temple for the Great Sun would come to be formed within her womb"** for in my sleep again did a figure of Holy Fire come close before me and tell me, **"By the Hand of God shall He be conceived within this women, the Chosen One from among the Temple Virgins, and to name him Jeshua."**

And so it now comes to pass that I am given to know your destiny to be that of a fisherman, not by trade but by the vision's spoken words **"by the Word of His Promise shall they fish for the souls of men within the seas of earth, and in His Name shall they cast their nets and find them full."** Having finished with the sharing of his visions, my father pulled me into his arms saying quietly, "I love you James"

That did not dismay my efforts to be a carpenter. In fact it enriched my desire to become better skilled and this I would eventually accomplish for I knew nothing of netting souls, nor was I fond of boats, and I was even less skilled as a swimmer. I had also noted that often the seas turn unfriendly in the blink of an eye. Many times in my life I questioned whether the Lord was wise in His choices, and as a young man I silently feared I would make no more a fisher of men than a carpenter.

Chapter 6

~ My Cup Runneth Over ~

There came a day in my twelfth year when I arrived home with a jar of water I was sent to fill, and I noticed my mother seemed to be anxiously awaiting me in the doorway. She took the vessel from my arms and beckoned that I sit in the place of my prayer. Softly, but in earnest, she bade me wash and clean my face and hands with the cloth and water she gave me. I did so with an urgency that pressed upon me, rendering me more curious than alarmed. She sat by the table, then, looking into my eyes, she said, **"My good son, you are blessed on this day. Your chores are done and you have earned your peace. Close your eyes and give yourself unto this prayer, that His Spirit you come to know and the Light of Truth be then your redeemer."** I trembled, for before my eyes could close she had turned to the window, whereupon there shone a growing brightness, greater than the daylight that now paled behind it.

Quickly I closed my eyes and fumbled in my mind for the prayer, but it was not forthcoming, for I was suddenly taken by the penetrating Light. Though I knew my body's eyes to be closed, I found there to be no darkness behind them, and it seemed natural that I could now see more clearly without them. And a man like Holy Fire stood before my mother and talked to her of things I could not hear, for it was not my place to hear them, though I knew them to be gifts and messages of Truth. And then came the prayer as if laid across my mind, and **down thru the crown of my head fell a single drop of Love Divine Force.** Though smaller than a grain of sand, it caused my body to become a tumbling river of rapturous joy that overflowed its banks. I was without and beyond myself, and could not comprehend such splendor and I succumbed to this most intense influence. So great and full was my bliss that inwardly I begged, "My Lord, let this River of Your Love go now forth from its place within me, for the sip from the Fountain of Your Heart I cannot contain within myself only. May it now comfort another, and even unto all others, such being the Will and Gracefulness of your Love."

In a short time I returned to my earthly senses but cared not to lift myself. I lay prostrate upon the ground, still blanketed in a peace not of this world and humbleness was large within my soul. I thought it a dream and desired not to awaken. I knew not what time had passed for the planes of the eternal are without time. My eyes opened at the sound of my mother's voice, **"James, awaken and rise, the sun is still noon brightness, and see how the candle has flickered but a few times. Praise the Goodness of His Spirit for He knew your prayer before you could speak it."**

For the rest of that day and the next, my body tingled with a delicious lightness and a perpetual tickle. I took great delight in the exquisite nature of this comfort that seemed to suspend my body and soul within a gentle waterfall of peace and joy. When Jeshua returned later that day he came straight to me and embraced me in silent affection. In that moment, with my eyes closed, I could not distinguish any space between us and then He gently whispered in my ear, **"Blessed are the pure of heart, for the Holy One reveals His Truth within you. As it has been written, "He Anoints my head with Oil and my Cup runneth over."**

It was a moment that I would always remember and carry within the recesses of my mind and heart. But over time, naturally, its brightness faded among the toils of earthly life and young manhood. But I was gratefully given to know that there exists the actual Living Love of our Creator, as a Great Force without Limits, and the Power to be Unimaginably Glorious.

Chapter 7

~ As a Boy, Jeshua Heals a Sparrow~

One day, as Jeshua and I played outside our home, a little sparrow limped upon the ground near us, and found its way to Jeshua's feet, and chirped sadly before us. Jeshua looked compassionately down upon the creature, then up at me and said warmly, **"Behold this innocent creature whom the Father has made to weave music upon the winds, to fly freely among the trees, if only to bring delight to the eyes and ears of men and children and even now is the Father's eye upon this little sparrow"** It had a feather on its back that awkwardly hung at its side and a leg that appeared bent or broken. Jeshua bent down and gently cupped the bird in his hands as it quietly chirped. He slowly brought the sparrow up to his chest, looked briefly to the heavens and then bowed his head, saying quietly, **"Be then restored to your perfect image and purpose; we give thanks for Your mercy and grace and by Thy will, let this be done."** The bird chirped loudly in His hands and He opened them, and the sparrow flew quickly into the air. Jeshua smiled broadly and I gasped in utter surprise, the words "Jeshua, oh, Jeshua" escaping from my lips.

He said only, **"Tell no one, James"** and we watched the bird disappear into the blue skies.

Chapter 8

~ Human Laughter, to ride the Breath of Joy ~

I found myself more strongly drawn to be near His side when no one else was present. I knew that when He was with me no harm could cross my doorstep, and this feeling was shared among his closest friends, family and, eventually, his followers. He shared certain secret things, intimately, that served to lift me into a state of awe, humility, and profound gratitude of heart, so that I thought this surely must be the promised savior of our nation.

Thus did he say to me, **"Such knowledge is open to all who would see, and are not secrets withheld by the Father from his Children. But man is not yet in the time of his Greater Understanding. He must first grasp the Heart of Love, for all other doors lead him astray from his Holy Temple. I give you these Pearls as blessings from the Father, for though your mind languishes in the mire of human concerns, your heart is strong in its conviction. By the spirit of compassion you have climbed the ladder of the soul, and are welcomed within the halls of Justice and Truth as a pillar in the Temple of the sacred meeting place between Heaven and earth. You will be known among your brothers as the just and righteous** one. **And with thy last breath you shall tell men the Truth that within man resides the Eternal Light of the Father, and the Father so loved His Sons that He sent His Way-Shower into the world as His Star of Love, and you knew Him not. But James, speak not to others of these Pearls I have given you lest they think them worthless stones of untruth and cast them into the dirt."** I quickly assured Him I would speak of it to no one and He smiled at me, amused, because I had thought to myself, "You draw enough attention from the wrong people without me stirring more dust into the wind!" He knew my thought, laughed and said **"Agreed my brother."** Over the years, I had learned what thoughts and comments would bring him to laugh and often with great vigor. He said, **"Human laughter is one of God's greatest gifts to Man for in that moment you are Freed of the World, and Ride a Breath of Joy."** I was grateful, for I felt it was something I could give to Him, who gave so much to others.

Chapter 9

~Joy and Work~

Jeshua greatly assisted my father when needed, always graciously and with great dedication to the task, while bearing a spirit of excitement and even joy. When a project was being performed in our home's shop, I was always gladdened by his presence, not just for the contribution he made with his natural abilities and understanding of the ways of carpentry, boat working, stone and metal work, but because it truly brought such deep delight to my father. It was amusing to both my brother and I to see how our father struggled not to show his joy at such moments, not wanting this to be felt by me as the favoring of one over the other. He truly was that beautiful a soul and man.

I would tease my father for amusement, in a manner that was also loving and respectful. "Father, do you see how Jeshua loves his work with you? Should you not be full of pride, for his skills and talents are so much more likened unto yours, and I am found to be so much the lesser?" My father replied, "James, you are not lesser...", and he hesitated in his words just long enough for me to say, "Father, I jest with you for I know you are more proud of me than my brother, who's lowly intent is only to show off and make himself to be greater than me." There was a pause which I filled with a smile. Then the three of us laughed at each other and ourselves.

Then I said to my father, "I know the fullness of your love for me and I am blessed in its comfort. So also am I filled with great contentment to be in your company and that of my brother. Fear not to be free and open with your joy my father, as both Jeshua and I would have you be so. We surely love and honor you." My father looked upon me with great love and pride, and nodded with appreciation. I then turned to Jeshua and said, "See that it is now true, I am the greater", and again we laughed. As we returned to our work, Jeshua added, as if thinking out loud, **"And he thinks he is not a fisher of men's hearts and souls?"**

He cast an all knowing smile and glanced at me and then to my father, who was beaming with happiness. I grinned, and confided to them my deepest felt sentiment, "I know this; there is not a greater brother to be found in all the heavens and the earth and I am blest." Jeshua then warmly replied, **"And thrice blest is he who looks to find the True Self in every brother."** I was given to thoughtful pause when my father spoke with kind authority, "Perhaps greater is the one that works more and speaks less." My brother and I both looked at him and each other, smiled, and nodded in agreement.

I tell you of these things so that you may know Jeshua very much cherished His daily earthly life, even saying, **"The greatest and simplest of gifts found within the human experience are those of Companionship, Love and Laughter, so I take great delight in the kindnesses that arise from the heart of Man, in his tender love of another."**

Chapter 10

~ A Mother's Love~

There came a day when I said to my mother, "I am troubled and ashamed before you because I have not the certainty of spirit that fills Jeshua. In His words I do believe and His manner I find endearing, so in great esteem do I hold my brother. I have even heard and seen wondrous things in His presence, yet do I falter in my faith for I am born of flesh and not like Him who was conceived by a Holy Breath. For what purpose would He have need of me? Should I not learn well the trade of my father who walks upright and is respected by men?" She took my hand and led me into our dwelling, taking a seat upon a pillow of blankets. She motioned that I should kneel and sit back upon my feet, whereupon she placed a lit candle between us, kissed once my forehead and spoke,

"**A mother's love is not without trial and woe. Though wisdom bathes her mind in lightness, so also may her heart be found heavy with the love of her children. To the things that I say, you shall listen and know them to be true. Do not judge yourself, neither let your brother be a yardstick by which you count your shortcomings, for you need only to**

love Him as you do now. Though He was not conceived by the seed of man, still He is born as a man, the same as you. He has chosen you, not for the weakness that befalls you, but for the purity and intentions of your soul. And you have chosen Him, yea, even from the Realms of Blessedness have you joined your brother's purposes. This much you may know and believe to be true. You need not fear, for He will never forsake you and will be near unto your side when you but call for Him. Love and comfort Him as a brother does and bring Him laughter, as is in your power to do. So also work hard beside your father, and learn and reap the gifts of his trade so that it can always sustain you in your responsibilities. And know always I give thanks unto the Father, for in these my children I am blessed among women."

In that moment I felt myself move beyond the fenced pastures and dreams of a boy. I had now stepped lightly onto the beckoning meadows of manhood that lay open before me. I stood up before her as she extinguished the candle. But before I could turn to the door, I heard the sound of her quiet tears, and always when she wept my breath took leave of me. There was a sad heaviness within my heart that seemed like a ship being cast downward by a great wave of sorrow, yet quickly I found myself wading into the widening seas of a much greater love. Instantly I reached for her and held her in tender love and silence.

Chapter 11

~ Jeshua interprets our cousin John's Dream, Elijah's Spirit has Come Again ~

Upon the shimmering shores of the Galilee Sea I would walk and watch the fishermen. Here also did my cousins, the brothers, John and James Zebedee, cast their nets in trade. They knew Jeshua, and from the beginning had heard the many stories that went between our families and friends: the whispers of His virgin birth coming in the time that a Great Star of fiery tail stretched across the heavens and sat overhead the hills of Bethlehem; the sound of angelic voices heard singing in the night of "the birth of a King and Savior", their heavenly echoes exclaiming "Peace and Goodwill to All Men ". And many more signs and omens were reported and shared among the devout of heart.

I recall an occasion when our families were gathered and my brothers and I, along with John and James, stood round a fire outside our home as the elders went inside to meet and offer prayer and thanksgiving. John, taking a deep breath soon asked, "Jeshua, my good cousin and brother, I am of mind to tell you of a dream that came upon me on the last night before we traveled here. I saw a man in the desert whose staff shone like silver fire. And there came a great lake that formed at his feet. And I saw multitudes of people who came to him, and he touched the waters with his staff and they became rich with sparkling stars, and the people followed him into the waters, for they were seen to be blessed by God. And then my eyes were cast upon a sandy hill to the east on which stood a giant whose head reached beyond the clouds, and his face shone like the sun and of whose stature I was in great awe. I thought him to be as a god; so were my eyes lowered in humbleness, when I heard a great fullness of voice saying, " **Arise, and behold the Pleasure of My Son."** And when I opened my eyes I saw now only the simple likeness of a man, yet one who walked upon still waters as if his feet had wings, and I marveled that he should come to greet me. And when I awoke, I suddenly knew him to look like you, were you a man of more years."

Jeshua took a breath of silence, then said, **"John, you are of my beloved and our families are in good sharing. Of this I can say, you have been blessed by the Lord for He has shown you a Holy vision and Spoken within your Soul. These visions are of things that are yet to come, and which you shall witness and find therefore to be true. So now has your vision been heard and shared amid these your brothers and cousins, so that they too may have strength of faith when they see these things shall come to pass. For the Spirit of Elijah has Come Again, this Harbinger whose staff shall stir the waters of men's souls, so that they may be readied and prepared to meet the Great Son of God who walks within their Holy Temple.**

So it is that all of you here are of His fold and will be given to follow in His Ways, that you should be freed from the bondages of the earth; to walk upon it, yet not be of it.

Marvel not that within the bosom of the Glorious Spirit of Our Father there lies a Love that would greet you at His Table ."

John was amazed by his interpretation and asked Jeshua, "And how shall we know of the coming of Elijah?" Jeshua replied, **"You will hear of a voice in the wilderness, crying "Prepare, for the Kingdom of God is nigh upon you. Be then cleansed of worldly things, that you may be filled by His Presence." You shall know his name also to be John, being that one who prays over men, saying, "In the Pure Waters of the Lord, you are found to be clean"."**

In that moment I knew the one He spoke of to be John, who studied together with Jeshua in the Temples of the Essenes. He was the only son of Elizabeth who had long been barren until his birth. My mother had told me once, **"The Messengers of the Lord had visited Elizabeth and given her Holy Word saying she would conceive a son of Great Spirit and Destiny."** I pondered these thoughts and, looking then at Jeshua, said nothing.

Chapter 12

~ Master Gardner, True Servant of the Most High ~

Jeshua at near nineteen years of age was soon to leave for what would be a long time, about ten years. He would carry with Him keen carpentry skills, and those of boat-working, metal and stone work and even weaving. But since His early years He had hungrily engaged Himself in study of the Jewish Scriptures, and also were the Temple Records of the Essenes laid open to Him. He had many discussions with learned men and women of upright heart who would serve to guide and nurture Him with their knowledge and wisdom. They were amazed and often humbled by young Jeshua's rapid understanding of all they had to offer. Even more so were they stunned by Jeshua's intense but sincere questioning and spontaneous interpretations of the sacred writings. These were instantly forthcoming from His lips the moment after reading a passage. His insights were deeply profound and greatly pondered upon within the hearts and minds of even the wisest of his teachers.

In the following, he gave the reasons for his leaving: **"Words are the arrows of thought. They are not themselves the**

Truth, but point man into the place of his deepest understanding. If a man would become a master gardener, then he must do more than just plant a seed. He must study the winds and the rains, the seasons, and the soil. So also must he know of the balance of sun and shade, and of all those things that work to bring forth a great harvest. He should seek for that knowledge in earnest and pray that the True Master Gardener be his teacher.

So also, if a man would become the Perfect Servant of God, he must do more than read only from those texts of his own people and lands. He must go further into the many Great Halls of Learning, for the Spirit and Wisdom of the Lord has visited all man and his ancestors. The student of Truth should gather for himself from all the Pearls of the Lord.

So I must journey to those places near and distant, even to the teachings within the temples atop the highest mountains and shrines to the East. Also shall I tarry among those secret and sacred passages lying deep within The Great Temples of the Sun in Egyptian lands, and along the shores and Labyrinths of Grecian wisdom. So shall I be about my Father's will.

In all these places are found Great Scrolls of Knowledge and I shall fill the basket of my soul with their bounty. But the greatest treasure to be found is in the understanding of all the toils and troubles that face every man of earthly incarnation and to know how I might serve to bring spiritual truth and freedom for the soul, heart, mind and body of mortal man, that he may clearly know for himself the path to the Father within. Then shall this Temple be readied for the greater increase of my Father's Spirit and Will, to be made manifest upon the Earth, for what is True Above must also be manifested Here Below.

Piercing the Veil of all the Kingdoms of Earth, the Heavens and throughout the stars, is the Light of Our Father's Love. This Presence and Spirit of Divine Love emanates from within the First Heavens of the First Cause of all Life, and may I come to be but a Temple Servant of The Most High, and therefore, True Brother to all my Brethren."

Privately he directed that I should stay close and tend to the needs of my father, who was aging, my mother, brothers and sisters. **"You will mature quickly in your manhood, and find the spirits of justness and fairness, mercy and compassion, to be your true nature. Then let it also be so in all your dealings with and among men. Become then the listener of your heart, and the pathway to giving true and good counsel will be opened."**

Chapter 13

~Being True to the Spiritual Self, above Earthly concerns ~

In the first few years following Jeshua's departure, there arose much gossip and discussion regarding His puzzling nature into which I was inevitably drawn, usually by request. By some it was begged of me to give answers to their questions, and they would ask me in a most humble and respectful fashion, and I did confide in them.

I was returning home with my father's tools in hand when a man, in a group of several, politely stepped into my path, saying, "James, son of Joseph the good carpenter, may you forgive my intrusion upon your path, but I am in vigorous discussion with these men regarding your brother. Surely you could tell us what you know to be true of him and bring resolution in a fair manner to us all?"

I did not wish to linger upon the streets as the sun would soon set and I was pressed to join my family. So I replied quickly, "I pray then that my assistance be of value, for it shall be the truth as I know it. But I must be brief, as I must tend to the needs of my father, mother, and kin, as is my honorable duty."

The man who sought my answers looked pleased and said, "Good, good, and so also have you honored us as your elders. So tell us, some say your brother was a spoiled child who used the scriptures as a means to escape work and be not the good son you are. Even now has he not shamed himself by abandoning the honor of his family and left upon a selfish journey? But I, my son, find no fault with your brother. I have watched and heard him with his friends since childhood. He seemed well beloved by all. Nor should he be looked down upon because he seeks truth within the pages of scriptures rather than the tool box of your father. Who can know with whom rests the calling of the Lord?"

Remembering my oath of truth, I began, "It is true that we all made great efforts to spoil Jeshua with our love and attentions and I would confide to you that it was exceedingly well received. It is true that He sometimes escaped heavy work beneath the hot sun as He effortlessly thumbed His time away with the turning of a scriptural page. It is also true He left on a journey with His meditations deeply centered within Himself, **to be true unto the spiritual self, even above all other duties and earthly concerns.**"

However, it is also true that He carried no shame at all for His behavior and thought not that He had ever dishonored any man. I would also agree with those who said, "Who can truly judge but the Lord?" I would be loath to do so, lest I dishonor my family and brother. I believe it also true that any man here would dishonor his Heavenly Father by taking the throne of judgment, as if it were his own. But I know you all to be respecters of the Lord and of His Perfect Knowledge and Judgment, so do I honor you, for you are found to be wise and humble men, which is undoubtedly heavily pleasing to the Lord. Now I must respectfully take your leave for I must be about my father's business." With that, I raised my father's tools and proceeded homeward with their perplexed stare fast upon my back.

As I walked I was given to reflect upon my answers to their questions. They sounded brilliant to me and I was puzzled as to how they fell into my thought and raced to my lips. Then I remembered what my brother once said: **"When you find you have snakes in your midst, first disarm their venom, walk freely into their hearts and then away from their den."** That was a basket full of wisdom I knew to always carry close around my neck. Along with, **"When men point at you and would cry evil things about you, cry back to them about a greatness within them that you know to linger near the surface of their heart, for when they point, now do you have their full attention."**

"Would it not be better to point over their heads crying "fire", and make quick haste thru the trees and bushes like our brother rabbit?" I said. He bent over with laughter, and replied, **"I cannot say if that would be the better, but I can see it to be a reasonable response and worthy of success, given the fleetness of your feet, which make you difficult prey. Remember not to stumble as you put great distance between yourself and them, so you can sleep well and see them in the morning."** Now it was I bent in laughter while crying, "But I would be discouraged to see them in the morning, How is that successful?" His reply, **"Well, I am assuming you would not trample on the rabbits?"**

I missed Him. But in my daydreams, I mused that perhaps He should not return. Could He not take a wife and raise children and find peace in a friendly and fertile land? Surely the Lord would find great merit in a simple life. Could not His dangerous visions naturally fade and be replaced with the love of a family? I pondered such thoughts quietly to myself, hoping God would place them into His Mind also.

Chapter 14

~ Simon and Andrew, the Kind Fishermen ~

I made friends of the many fishermen and their families and often I would trade services for fresh fish to put upon our table. Among the fishermen were the brothers Simon and Andrew who were raised to inherit their father's boats and nets. They seemed more persistent and confident than many who fished beside them, and the harvest of their efforts was more fortunate. It was by my cousin John that I came to know Simon and Andrew. John had come to me saying I could find work and trade for fish by helping in the repair of boats along the banks.

John led me along a weaving trail of people, nets, boats and baskets. Then he stopped and I saw that his eyes were upon the waters. "There." He pointed. "They return. Let us go down to meet them." As the boat neared the shore a young man with black hair, skin darkened by the sun, girt in a loincloth, his form strong and sturdy, dropped into the shallow water and took hold of a rope and pulled the bow onto the sand. Small bands of children gathered around him begging for fish and the man called out to his brother, "Andrew, have we fish or just weeds and rocks to share?" The children's eyes were alight with excitement, for they knew when Simon teased them he had fished well and would be generous to the poor of his people. Andrew stood in the boat and replied, "I would say we have plenty of both," and he paused, "of rocks and weeds that is." He smiled as the children's hopes spilled into giggles of joy, for they knew this brother to also jest in times of plenty. He then raised a readied basket from the boat's floor and down into their small hands, which together they took good hold of and gave great thanks to the fisherman and praised the blessings of the Lord.

These were men of compassion and dedicated workers for the betterment of all. This Simon and his brother reminded me of something Jeshua once said: **"Consider the purity of the man who's greatest joy is found in those things that bring gladness to his child's heart, so also is this the Way, Truth and Life of your Heavenly Father, the Rock and Foundation of Your Spirit and Temple."**

"Simon and Andrew," John began, "This is my cousin I spoke of, James, son of Joseph the carpenter and Mary." Reaching for Simon's hand, I said, "I am pleased to be in your company. I see you fished well today, and may I honor you for the spirit and manner of your generosity. That was a beautiful gift for me to behold."

Simon's eyes pierced mine, studying their sincerity, and then he said, "James, I am also honored to meet a man that is sensitive to the character of another. Your words are generously filled with kindness. I would embrace your hands but I fear I would soil you with fish oil." I replied, "Fear not, my feet are already lost to scales and slime, and now the smell follows me everywhere. Perhaps women will shun me? Have you found this to be true?" We laughed, then Andrew said, "I too am glad of your company and that you are already fouled with fish, because now you can commence with their cleaning." A basket of fish landed in my arms so suddenly I almost dropped it. I blurted out as I shook my head, "And I thought I was pleased to come here? I must have walked in the sun for too long and my good sense has taken flight of me!" Thus, in laughter, there was formed a good and friendly bond between us and a wave of respect passed through our souls.

Chapter 15

~My Brother Jude~

Soon I brought Jude into their midst, so that he too became their friend. I would come to know and honor these men deeply, and love how they would one day love Jeshua, my Eldest brother. Jude was a good and obedient child and tender brother. He was so exuberant in his play with his children friends that he required great naps at its conclusion, and to rouse him was amusingly difficult. "Jude, Jude wake, you have much more play to do." I jiggled his leg and he pulled it away. "But Jude, all the girls are here at your door and wish to play with your hair. Would you disappoint them?" "Enough James," my mother sighed. "He is not old enough to appreciate your jesting and may kick you like a mule." We laughed quietly and let him sleep and I henceforth tried to resist my desire to tease him, though not always successfully.

When I became more my father's helper, Jude inherited the chores of the home and the needs of our mother. I would always feel protective of him, yet he never seemed to need shielding. He would learn some of the skills of our father and would fish with his cousins James and John. But during the time of Jeshua's great journey and learning, Jude enjoyed the workings of the market place, taking delight in the correct measuring of grains, grapes, fish, wool, skins and cloth materials. He combined his natural fairness and personable skills of trade. He was as energetic in his work as he was in his childhood play, and women preferred and sought his company and attentions over other traders. Jeshua had also taken special time with him, guiding him in his understanding of the spiritual laws of life, his place on earth, and his services to both God and men. However, Jude, early on, was not inclined to believe in the rumors surrounding his oldest brother and was respectfully uninterested in talk that placed Jeshua on a mission from God. But of course, that would eventually change.

Chapter 16

~Born Captains of God, Sailing the Sea of Love~

For the many years that Jeshua was about his Father's purposes in the distant lands of his travels, I would often see him in dreams. In one such sleeping vision I saw his form on a great desert. I called to him and tried to hasten to him, but my feet seemed heavy, slowed by the sand and I feared I would lose him. I then beheld a great chasm between us and I was stricken with grief and the fear that I would see him no more. I was calling hard upon the Lord, praying that it would not be so, when I heard my brother's voice near to me. **"James, it is I."** I opened my eyes and saw that he walked across a small stream lying just before me, upon rocks flat and worn smooth. He then embraced me saying **"Fear not"** and I nearly fainted with relief as great peace and joy overtook me. I immediately awoke to find the great cloak of His presence fast around me, and I gave humble thanks for his assurance was still full within my senses.

 I knew then that Jeshua had some mastery within the planes of earth for no time or distance held or ruled him. I often wondered what powers he possessed, or , whether, perhaps, the power of the Divine possessed him as it possesses us all and I was reminded of his words: **"Hear, O Israel, the Lord thy God is One. All Life is the Body of God. What we see to be real are the many faces of created form but, in Truth, there is only the Creator with all Form bearing His Life and Force. The Spirit of the Father-Mother Creator is the Foundation of our Soul. The Greatness of His Light within us can never be destroyed. Therefore our journey is assured to be always perfect in Him.**

Divine Love and Eternal Companionship are the gifts of Our Creator. We are in Holy Covenant with Our Father. We are His Light and the Life-Filled Stars of His Love. You are Sons and Daughters of a Wondrous Light whose Great Self desired you Come Forth to be With Him in Perfect Companionship in the Eternal Experience of Creation.

Your Souls are Brilliance in Motion. You were born as Captains of God that you may sail the Greatness of His Seas of Love. You are the Father's Firstborn Thought and Desire, the Sparks of the Creative Forces issuing from the Throne of Blessedness. You are More than all Man combined, Greater than none, and there is No Lesser among you. But these are not the things a person sees and knows unless his heart seeks to give spacious room and honor to the knowledge of his Father's Presence.

So also is it true that a person may have no understanding of his heavenly origins and no concept of a God, yet lives by that very same Spirit of love and compassion, kindness, and the forgiving of self and others. These too are the pure handiwork of God."

Chapter 17

~Father, Your Work is Well Accomplished~

My most beloved father had gradually become weakened in his body. But suddenly one day he could not raise himself from his bed. His skin looked gray and I deeply grieved for I knew he would depart this world soon, maybe in days. He was not lucid at all times and we all stayed near. My family, all here in our home, consisted of three sisters, Ruth, Miriam and Martha, and brothers Jude, Joseph and Simon, all of whom loved him dearly. My mother fed him what he would eat which was little. I saw my mother's tears fall on him, many of them, so many I could not count, for I became blinded by my own.

I honored, loved and respected this man more than any man I would ever know. I knew I could never fill his shoes, and he humbled me in my every part. I had never heard an unkind word leave his lips. I had seen him brought to anger, though always appropriate and with good reason. Yet he never lashed out but would choose his words wisely and sincerely, and sternly only if needed.

He dedicated his life to his family with all that was within him. His life was hard and arduous, yet we heard him say every rising of the morning sun, "I am blessed among men and give thanks my Lord for my cup is full and no greater treasure found than that of my beloved wife and children, whose love surrounds my table and brings comfort to my heart and soul."

I would miss hearing those words, and only now do I realize the sound of his prayer was the tender music of his soul. In the whispered softness of his voice I heard the winds of courage. I sensed the bow of his faith being like the strength of a tree, and the purity of his heart resonated with the gentleness of his beloved spirit. Indeed, I knew his prayer to be a precious melody of gratefulness for the love that filled his sails. A finer father and husband could never be found. A great inspiration from the Throne of God was this man Joseph.

On the second morning came the moment of his passing. I had been vigilant to his needs and my mothers and been awake for all this time. I was sitting on my blanket in my place of prayer and resting against the wall. I saw there was a slight lightening in the darkness outside and I was glad for I thought to myself, "The sun will soon rise and help keep me wakeful." I then fell fast asleep and knew not that I had done so. I dreamed thus: I saw Jeshua enter the doorway. The sun that had risen behind Him filled the room with a golden light. He stepped before my father's bed and opening His arms He said, **"Father, your work is well accomplished. Would you rise now and come with me to see Paradise again?"**

Suddenly I awoke. My eyes darted to my father, his head being cradled in my mother's hands, and in her look I knew my father had departed from his body. I hastened to her side and though I was ashamed for sleeping and deeply saddened, I pleaded to my mother, "Tell me Mother, did he say anything before he passed? I must know." She lifted her eyes to mine and nodded. "Yes" she said, "Just moments ago, He opened his eyes suddenly and smiled, saying "Yes, with this Sun I will arise", and in that instant did the breath of his spirit pass from him."

I cried, "Mother, I saw Jeshua here. I know I was asleep but I saw clearly Jeshua came for him, to take him from the suffering of the body and lift him into heavenly places. I give thanks to the Lord for showing me this Truth." My mother replied, "I saw Him too, but only through the look I beheld in your father's eyes when he spoke those words, and now I am pleased to hear that your eyes were opened and this sign given to us. So may we all find peace this day in the merciful workings of the Lord."

Chapter 18

~John the Baptizer and the Blind Man's Vision~

One day my cousin John came to visit. He was excited to tell me he had heard from Simon. "There is word of a teacher and holy man in the desert who speaks boldly of a new kingdom being at hand. They say he has the look of the wild, being clad in camel fur. So James, John continued, perhaps we should go to see for ourselves this man and see what message he offers and if it be of merit?" For a brief moment I puzzled to myself, "Could this be Jeshua who returns in a wild manner and dressed in camel fur!?" Suddenly John said, as if knowing my thoughts, "But I must also tell you his name is said to be John and I remember the dream your brother interpreted many years ago, saying Elijah would come again and his name would be John. "Yes, of course", I replied quicker than I intended, but I was swept upon a current greater than myself. I knew I was to go see this man.

So John, Simon and I sailed to the southern end of the Galilee Sea, and from there followed a lengthy path along the river Jordan to a bend near Jericho. Word had spread quickly of a strange prophet who came forth from the desert and was now baptizing the people. It was said that he preached that one should become clean of the darkness that binds from within, and to ready ourselves for the Kingdom of God is close upon us. Along our journey, John and I spoke of John's dream from some years before and together we shared his vision and Jeshua's interpretation with Simon.

Eventually, we encountered many other curious and hopeful souls along the road. But there is one engagement that I shall never forget. There was a man, an old man, thin and worn of body, blind from birth, and he carried a staff in one hand and in his other, the hand of the young boy who led him. Tears like a gentle rain washed his sunken, bearded face. He was thanking the Lord for "the Vision of the Light without darkness". His voice was not loud, like that of a braggart, rather I found the thankfulness in his voice attractive to my ear, for each word he spoke carried a breath of deep and genuine sincerity. I paused, and my comrades as well, and I said unto the man, "Elder and brother, may I implore of you, what is it that you have seen? Have you been to the place of the prophet and baptizer?" "Yes," he replied. "Let us rest a moment together."

In a shaded spot we sat and the voice of the blind man began: "John is the name of this prophet, and the sound of his words brought hope into my heart. I went to him in humble petition that my sins be forgiven, that I be cleansed of my darkness, so that I too might be found within the Light of God and given entrance into His Heavenly Kingdom. Then did he pass me beneath the waters of baptism saying, **"You are received by your Father and by the Graciousness of His Mercy, you are delivered into the Kingdom of the Holy One where His Light shall dispel all darkness."**

I had then taken rest beneath a tree, and knew not if I slept, when I suddenly found myself held within a gentle whiteness of

Light that brought great and heavenly peace within my soul as if my eyes could see, and I heard a great voice say, **"You shall call upon the Light of my Son who will give thee earthly sight."** Suddenly I awakened from this wondrous vision and began giving true praise unto the Spirit of God whom I had seen dwells in a Perfect Light for He had opened His door within me and I was humbled and waited upon His Word to be fulfilled, that I should be blind no more. Then certain followers of this prophet and baptizer took word to him that I had seen a great vision, and he came before me saying, **"Thus has the Lord heard the prayer of the truly repentant, and the Messiah and Savior shall soon come with great power and loose the shackles of man's blindness and the infirmities that bind him in darkness. Return then to your home in Jerusalem, having faith that the coming Restorer of the Kingdom of God shall find you. And that the glory of God may be manifested before men, the Promised One will loosen the scales from your eyes and you shall praise the Lord your God for all your days and even beyond this world shall you gladly serve His Will."**

Thus I have told you the truth of what I have seen and heard. Though not with earthly senses have I come to know these things but with the eyes and ears of a spirit that I now see as living within me. Some have whispered that perhaps I am mad as well as blind, saying that some demon has possessed my mind. But I care not, for I have seen and been given remembrance of one great truth, that I am forever in the hands of a Great Light who bathes my soul in a perfect Love."

I lightly grasped the man's arm, saying, "Fear not, your words ring with true conviction and I am grateful for hearing them." And Simon said, "Perhaps it is we who are the blinder, for now it is you who truly sees what human eyes cannot." And he thanked the man for the testimony of his baptism. John gave the blind man and the boy a share of bread, water and a coin and thanked them saying, "Your story I find both inspiring and intriguing. I pray your journey home is safe and well-lit by every star in the heavens of the Lord." "So be it," we all agreed.

We traveled on until early evening, built a fire for warmth on a sandy patch along the river's path, slept until early dawn and then proceeded to our destination. It was late afternoon when we rounded a bend and saw a group of a hundred or so men, women and children, various tents and several fires for cooking and warmth. My eyes fell upon the figure of a tall, muscular, sun-darkened man, wrapped in animal skins, the furs giving him the imposing look of an upright lion. He stood upon a slab of smooth rock that rose out of the river near its edge. The waters here danced ever so lightly and sparkled behind him.

A crowd of people sat or stood before him. He spoke in a bellowing voice, rich with a spirit of authority that caused my ear to listen deeply. I quietly divined within myself that this voice carried Messages from the Most High, and this bright and fiercely imposing man was indeed anchored in Truth. He held a great wooden staff in his hand which he now pointed into the crowd, and then, raising it, aimed it firmly at the sun. John looked upon the scene before him and whispered out loud, "This is remarkable, so much in the manner of my dream." Simon stepped past us, saying, "Come brothers, let us go among them and see and hear for ourselves if this be truly a prophet of the God of Israel."

Simon and John pressed quickly ahead of me. I needed a moment to reflect on why I suddenly seemed hesitant to move my feet forward. My heart pounded out an excited but nervous rhythm, and for a brief moment I thought to myself that perhaps, if I stopped here, I would stop other events from unfolding, those prophetic visions of mayhem and crucifixion confided to me by my brother Jeshua, many years ago. Suddenly John turned and seeing I was not behind him, he stopped, searched around him and then looked up to where his eyes met mine. I sighed and immediately proceeded down to join him and Simon.

"The man who is not repentant, is also the prisoner of a darkness that binds him, for he holds fast to heavy doors that enclose him in worldly illusions that have become his god." cried this John the baptizer. "Has not the Lord of the Heavens said plainly, "I Am that I Am and Let no other gods stand before Me"? Heed then the Spirit of the Everlasting One whose Perfect Kingdom resides within your Temple. Repent of your sins of selfishness and greed.

Follow not the ways of the unmerciful and unrighteous, nor be one who wrongfully judges others, while thinking you are greater or favored in the eyes of the Lord. Be not like those viperous serpents who are filled with all manner of uncleanliness, and who conceal the bones of wolves beneath their priestly robes and kingly attire. They that hide behind the raiment of their earthly stature know not the path that would bring them entrance into the Holy of Holies, the very Light of God that illumines the soul, heart and mind of man from within.

Forgive one another for the many transgressions you have committed and those against you, and so shall you find the Light of Redemption within you, the Father and your Truth.

Prepare your Temples in Purity, for soon comes the Promised Deliverer of the Kingdom of Heavenly Light upon the earth. Hasten to find yourself among those readied for entrance into this Kingdom. Behold the Gates of Heaven open wide before you. The proud shall be humbled while the meek shall be lifted by the coming of a True King. A

great Sun and Star of the Spirit of Our Father God, whose Truth rules the Heavens and the earthly realms and worlds, shall bring a Light that shall shine into all the corners of the earth and for the many ages to come.

Look within your past and for all your days be repentant of those transgressions you committed against your neighbor, who is also your brother and sister, your mother and your father. Make way for the Waters of Love to fill your Spirit and bring you peace even in the face of the storms of life. Come all those who hear my voice, be baptized in the Pure and Holy Waters that surround you and give praise and thanks for the Lord who would soon free your souls from the heavy yoke of your afflictions and earthly bonds."

I was spellbound. I proceeded no further as Simon and John pressed thru the crowd to get closer to the man and prophet whose voice gripped me. His words sparked hope and wonderment in the minds and hearts of our people, his people. Our nation thirsts for news of the Promised King who will surely bring us deliverance from Roman tyranny. Many believed that God would establish His Kingdom of Heaven among us, being His chosen people, raising our nation above all others. I also yearned for our people's redemption. Would not the Kingdom of God bring justice and mercy as a cornerstone of its power and authority, and bring peace to this our land? I wish no ill of these Gentiles, if only that they be dissuaded from controlling our lives and our borders, and return to their own lands.

But there is another tyranny that haunts me, that being our own Sanhedrin, the Temples of Priests and Judges who command that our attentions give honor to their stature before God and be submissive to their word or whim. I do not trust any man who would callously condemn an adulteress to be stoned for being but human or give their blessing to painful lashings for the smallest of crimes.

Too often they would nod their head to the accusers, as if God Himself had made true judgment through them, but I never saw any trace of the Light of God behind such darkness and cruelty and many of them I did not believe to be true servants of the Spirit of the Lord. Jeshua once said to me, **"You shall know a man's true station within the Mansions of Life and Love Divine by the fruit of his branch and the thoughtful manner of his actions, for when he offers a tender word or helpful hand to his brethren in true Mercy and Compassion, to the Guilty as well as the Innocent, then know his roots are strong in the Garden of the Lord who so receives His Children Equally, in Grace and Mercy and Without Pause."**

While my mind had thus drifted, I saw now that a group of about ten people had entered the shallow waters around the baptizer, and among them stood both Simon, who had impulsively removed his robes and stood clad only in his loincloth, and my cousin John, who remained robed and looked to be in a state of great awe. For those who were baptized while clothed, the baptizer produced from his skins a large half of a shell and spilled its contents slowly on their heads, while speaking quietly to each one. Simon, and another man dressed in a loincloth, he submerged completely and quickly, and then poured water from the shell over them, speaking to them in the same quiet manner.

I did not share their immediate compulsion to be baptized, though I was highly enamored by his words and felt this John likely to be a true Messenger from God and for our people. After he had finished his conversions with water and prayer, he walked to a shady space among a grove of trees followed by a small group of men, Simon and my cousin John among them. I joined them by taking a seat just behind my cousin and Simon who both turned and greeted me with a smile and a nod. The baptizer sat against a tree, his spine straight, shoulders back, and crossed his legs upon his lap; closed his eyes, bowed his head slightly and remained motionless and seemingly breathless for several minutes.

In the meantime, Simon began quietly pressing John to tell the baptizer of his dream and of the interpretation given by my brother.

Finally, Simon, almost begging John, said, Ask him if he is the prophet Elijah, who has come again." In that moment the baptizer raised his head and looking first at Simon and then to John he said," Speak, my brother, and tell me what presses upon your mind."

My cousin, addressing John the baptizer as Rabbi, told the story of his dream and how Jeshua had said it was a vision of the coming of the spirit of Elijah. There was a murmur and gasp of awe that circled those who were gathered with us. Then John quickly ended his story with, "Are you then the Elijah of my vision?" To which he replied, **"I am one whose voice cries in the desert to make way for the coming of a Great King whose sandals I am not worthy to wear and who shall bring the Light of God among men and to every nation. His word shall cover the earth, even to the end of the ages. Ask not by what name I now bring you this message, rather humbly implore your Heavenly Father that you might find your name as it is already so written upon the scrolls of His Heavenly Kingdom, and give thanks, for the gift of His Love has set itself within your journey. My name is John, as it was so given."**

This is indeed the prophet Jeshua spoke of, I thought to myself. And if it is my brother he speaks of, this prophet calls him a Great King. But my brother denied he would rule upon the earthly throne of Israel, saying **"My place is not of this world, but in the finer realms of the my Lord and Father."** Such things like these troubled me.

Chapter 19

~Jeshua Returns~

Soon after the return journey, my family received word thru a traveling merchant that Jeshua was soon to return. He refused a token coin saying, "I was most generously compensated by Jeshua and I could accept no more. For a while we traveled together. I found him to be deeply engaging. His manner and presence felt much like a comforting breeze on a desert trail. Your pride is rightly placed in this your son and brother."

Three days later, Jeshua returned. Our mother, brothers, and sisters shared tears in a joyous spirit of great love and deep gratefulness. Jeshua held each one of us for what seemed a long time and so deeply felt were our emotions that few words could escape our mouths, except the cry or gentle moan of thankfulness that occupied our breath.

He came and held me last. I was shaking. He pulled me close, saying, **"My tender brother, I could not be prouder of the care of our family that you have provided so nobly and generously. The Lord our Father blesses our family thru you for your heart has prayed to be His servant and for His will to be done on earth, and so has it come to pass. Know that**

His Seed within you lies also in the Garden of His Heart so that your Soul may flourish in the Rain and Light of that Perfect Love and Spiritual Presence." He turned to the family, saying **"Peace now be with us all on this blessed moment of our reunion, and I give thanks unto my Lord and Father for His blessings are great and many."**

Chapter 20

~Jeshua Baptized~

"James", He whispered near my ear as we lay preparing to sleep, "We shall soon go to honor the Spirit of our Father within the baptizer, John, for he is a great and Pure Servant of God. I shall be baptized like any man, and would bid you follow as well, my brother."

And so we went to the place of John's preaching and baptisms. I slowly followed Him into the waters. When He stepped before John, I stopped and found myself taking steps backwards, as if pulled by an unseen force. Suddenly there was quietness. The birds were silent, the rolling noise of the river seemed to dissolve into a hushed pool of wavy glass, and time stopped, for there came upon and around Jeshua the Light of the Eternal, a great and Holy Brilliance, yet it did not suffer my eyes to behold it and I found myself on my knees. Then a Great and Wondrous Voice filled the air, the countryside, and all the world, and I marveled at it. **"Behold the Pleasure of My Blessings, brought forth in this My Son who bears My Heart and Spirit. Receive Him and the Crown of Love and Truth He brings to all, in My Name."** As John poured water over Jeshua's head, there appeared wings of a Holy Fire, that held the likeness of a candle flame in its center and, like an angelic bird, it rested upon Jeshua's head. John bowed his head as Jeshua embraced him and kissed him gently upon his cheek and moved toward the shore. I stood upon trembling legs and moved to come before John. He then lifted his head as I dropped to my knees in the waters, whereupon he poured water from his shell over my head, saying, **"Blest are you James, brother of the Sun of Love, as it is in the heavens so be it now on earth. Be then faithful to His purposes, grow in faith and wisdom and repent of your weaknesses by forgiving them in others."**

I returned to my family without Jeshua. He had told me when I joined Him on the shore of the river that He had to withdraw into the desert for a time to fulfill His Father's purposes, and to **"fear not for me for my path is well lit"**. I spoke of these things with my mother, saying, "I have seen the hand of God upon Jeshua, as surely as I see my own. I was humbled, and even afraid. Am I not blest among men, yet I am unnerved. Where is the weakness of my faith that I question the Will of God who has opened my eyes to His Light and my ears to His Great Voice which resounds around and within me? Mother, your son Jeshua surely comes from God, but I shamefully fear to what end." Her eyes were full of tender love and an understanding that what I was coming to know was well anchored in unearthly wisdom.

"James, my good son, you are no less a man because you care for your brother. Your fears are but the shadows of your earthly mind and are loosened from their chains to assault you in this way. It is the love of your brother that sets these thoughts aflame. You will one day rise beyond them and you shall be freed of these lingering chains and fear no more. You are neither disloyal to God nor your brother. Over time, we all grow in the Light of our faith in God's Will. Thank

you, James, for having gone with Jeshua and for being a true witness of this baptism of Holy Fire. Let us now give thanks for the gifts of God that have fallen upon our doorstep."

And when He returned, I knew He was changed, and would always be so, for as long as I would know Him. He was, or seemed, Larger, yet Lighter. He emanated a peaceful, loving Presence, and a deep spirit of humility. Several times I heard Him prayerfully whisper, **"I am Humbled before Your Light, My Father. Thy Will be then Our Journey"**.

Chapter 21

~Evil never truly was, except as a Compass for the Soul ~

In the late of day, with the sun having just set below the hills, I sat with Jeshua and His chosen apostles. We gathered about Him while He skillfully, powerfully, and graciously answered our many questions. Peter, saving his question until all the others had finished, finally asked, "Jeshua, tell us, what is man to God?" Thus did He answer, **"Peter, and my brothers, truly I tell you that we are the Great Brotherhood of the Soul, the Living Reflections of the Most High. We are a Great Pearl without price which knows no death."** Jeshua then raised Himself to stand among us. I felt as though something was about to happen, as if some door or tunnel was opening around us, and I braced myself as He said, **"Upon the Eternal Planes of Spirit there resonates the Song and Praise of the True Heart of our Brotherhood. I bring it before the ears of you righteous men that you now may find remembrance of this Truth. Close your eyes and give yourself into prayer."** And Jeshua, closing His eyes, prayed with a voice of inner radiance, and there came upon us all a heavenly light as He spoke the words,

"We will wait upon the Lord for before His Glorious Face we have stood in the Light of His Ecstasy; there, where our Halls filled with the wonderment of His Sight, so making our legs to tremble and falter. So great was our Awe and beyond full our Humility that Lo, we did leave our heart upon His Doorstep. Thus do we wait upon our Lord for He is the True Father and the Shepherd of our Spirit and Soul. We have seen our many gods fall before Him, and found welcomed sanctuary within this Magnificent Heart of Divine Vastness and Love without Measure. Here shall we serve the Lord, for His will is ever perfect, His goodness our staff. We are all servants of the Truth and Spirit of The Eternal One."

Each of us found our spirits to be caught up in the Light of a Divine Presence. But only for myself can I speak. I saw a flash, like white gold-fire and brighter than the sun, pierce the crown of my head. I saw that scales fell from my eyes and were cast to the ground. I remembered these to be the tools of illusion, the shadowy substance of the Veil. I beheld Jeshua's True Self as being The Heart and Presence of my Heavenly Father, and I knew this to be the Same Truth within myself and within all, and then came a Peace beyond words. I was stripped clean of all thought, and consumed in a rapturous understanding of The Perfect Goodness of all Life, Now and Forever. And while I was held in this Light of Truth I saw and knew there was No evil to exist. Then as the Light of this Heavenly Presence withdrew, we each found our eyes to be opened and I beheld Jeshua to have a great aura of light surrounding Him. Above His head were luminous transparent bands of purple, then gold, then white. I knew these manifestations reflected the Purity of the Mind, Heart and Soul that dwelt within this His body Temple. And then his words being few, he said, **"Thus are you given to know of, and believe in He that sent me."**

I did indeed believe he was sent from the Maker. And this experience brought inner transformation. A great question that lay hidden within me was suddenly revealed and divinely answered. Long had I silently pondered in my breast, "Why must the Lord allow so much bad and evil to exist and the suffering it creates? Is there any true Justice to be found upon the earth?" But now, having miraculously passed from the veils of earth into the Presence and Knowledge of a Holy Truth, I can bear true witness to the Perfect Stream of All Life, and that His Goodness Reigns King and is Without Shadow. Evil never truly was, except as a Compass for the Soul.

But life in the body looked and felt real enough to me and I was fully immersed in its challenges. Those spiritual experiences that came by my Father's Hand were intense and took me to realms beyond the body. But so also were they brief and I soon found myself to be my human self once more. However, I retained the unshakable knowledge that there is the Presence of the Creative Spirit of the Father by which We Live, Move and Have Our Being, and we are indeed forever blest. That was of immeasurable assistance but did not make me invincible in the world, only more attentive to everything in it.

Chapter 22

~The Blind Man~

He sat upon a blanket on a street in Jerusalem, as he did every day, with his cane and small basket beside him, begging for alms to satisfy his meager needs. The morning sun bathed him in a welcomed warmth as he prayed quietly for the mercy and grace of his God to bless all who passed him, whether they were able to share a coin or not. Having lived in darkness since birth, he had grown accustomed to the rigors of the life afforded him and his dependence on the kindness and mercy of others had left him always in a state of gratefulness and humility. He whispered his prayers quietly to himself, when suddenly his ears took notice of rising voices, calling "Rabbi, do tarry with us for we are hungry for your words."

His head cocked in attention, he sensed a small crowd approaching and pushed himself onto his knees to better hear what the commotion was about. Suddenly his heart began to pound with anticipation, for there came within him that same lightness that had befallen him the day the baptizer John had poured water over him and he cried, "Rabbi, Rabbi, have mercy on me, for all my days I have not seen the light of this world with my eyes, but only now my heart wakens in a Light I understand not, but it comes in your footsteps; hear me Rabbi, forsake me not, You are the Promised One, please take pause before me, my Lord my God has quickened my heart. Would thou find me worthy within His Kingdom?" Tears filled his eyes as he trembled now breathless, for he heard and felt the crowd stop before him. **"Good brother"**, Jeshua said softly. **"Would you now see clearly the world before you, the light that surrounds you, the sun, moons and stars, the faces of those who care for you, here within the mansion of the Father of Life? Upon this earth He has carried your soul and body thru these difficult struggles, and behold has your Heavenly Father indeed found you a worthy Son within His Kingdom. I bring His Light to the doorstep of your heart, my friend, and you shall know joy, in fullness this day."** "Let it be then as you have said," sobbed the blind man. "Let His will be my comforter and finally my peace." Jeshua knelt before him, taking earth and sand from the street, and with his hand he caught tears that fell like rain from the blinded eyes and did make a salve in His palm. **"Now, the Light and Love of God shall be visited upon you"**, said Jeshua, as He pasted the damp mix over his sightless eyes, **"Go now to the pool and wash the darkness from your eyes forever, and tell no man who has done this for you, except that it could only be God the Father and Mother of Holy Light."** A kind young boy then led him to the waters, wherein he did wash the salve from his eyes, and the blind man cried out, "Lord, I can see, Your Glory now breaking the scales from my eyes." He reached to touch his reflection and saw the sparkle of the Sun on the water and the astonished face of his young helper who now fell to his knees and lightly laid his hand upon the shoulder of the man, his friend, who now was no longer blind.

Chapter 23

~The Adulteress~

One day while walking with Jeshua and several of his apostles thru the sandy streets of Jerusalem, we were confronted purposefully by a group of six men, several of them being temple priests, who roughly dragged a severely distraught woman with them. They shoved her down onto the dirt at the feet of Jeshua, saying, "This woman bears the stench of the sin of adultery for we took her from the soiled bed of another man. Behold her husband who suffers from this ungodly defilement and walks with us to deliver the just punishment of her crime, as written in the word of our people's laws that decree she must now be stoned. What say you Jeshua, would you also agree the Laws of God must be followed?"

Thus the trap was set, for these priests would report Jeshua's response as proof of her guilt, and the death sentence would be carried out. But, deceitfully, what they inwardly sought, was for Jeshua to part ways with the Holy Books, giving them reason to have the Temple guards arrest him for the breaking of Jewish law. The poor woman cried desperately at His feet for mercy. I was sickened with fear and disgust at the cruelty against her.

Without a word, Jeshua bent down and picked up a stick that lay beside the woman, looked up at the gathering of her accusers, and proceeded to weave His way thru them. Taking the stick in His hand He wrote in the sand, before the feet of each of them, a name, and each name differed from the rest. The men turned pale as they saw the name, so uncomfortably personal to them, that instantly brought them to recall their own sins, secretly hidden from themselves and others. The husband, who had been forcing this wife to sell her body for his own selfish purposes and greed, looked down on the name at his feet and was aghast, for the name was that of a woman whom he secretly visited and lusted to make his wife, and could do so, once this wife was dispensed with. Jeshua looked down upon the woman and spoke only the words, **"Let he that is without sin, be then the first to cast their stone.'**

One by one, the guilty men and priests dropped their stones and scurried away, abandoning their cruel mission. Gently, Jeshua lifted the sobbing woman and held her in His arms, saying **"Where are your accusers now, good woman?"** She cried out, "They are all gone, my Lord, by the mercy of God, they have left me! Am I thus forgiven?" Jeshua wiped the tears from her face with his robe, softly saying, **"I find no fault in you"**. Henceforth did this woman gratefully and humbly follow Jeshua and his disciples, desiring only to be of pure and noble service to the God of Mercy and Grace. This instance was a wondrous miracle to have witnessed, the beauty and tenderness of which I would never forget.

Chapter 24

~ Every Man is the Temple of God, and His Soul, the Portal of Divinity ~

One evening my brother and I sat outside our home taking refuge in the coolness of the night. The stars seemed brighter and the air clearer and crisp with late summer sweetness. I pondered the skies quietly to myself until I broke the silence. "Jeshua, I have often looked upon these heavens, the vast and numberless stars that encircle the earth, and wondered what messages and grand purposes they must hold. If they are placed by the Perfect Hand of God, then would not each one be important? And I know not why, but I feel as though they can see me much clearer than I see them. They seem to me to be Eyes that peer down into my every thought, word and deed. I feel no threat and am instead comforted by the sense that I have a vast and loyal family all about me. I marvel deep in my temple that all these things, the beauty of the heavens and earth, are but doors to the Great Mind of God and the wonderment of His Heart. And though my senses fill with joy and admiration of my Father's Painting of Life, I am saddened by a longing that I cannot fill. What is it Jeshua, that calls from deep within me that I know not how to answer?"

My brother pulled a blanket across us to contain our warmth in the gathering chill of the night air. In a moment I knew from the sound of His breathing that He was given to prayer. I knew to wait and not interrupt His communion for I felt great reverence for His time of prayer, be it long or short. I was blessed by these moments and I would often follow Him in my spirit and I perceived He was neither begging nor in supplication of the Lord. Instead, He emanated the aura of the surrendering of His human self to be joined in communion with the True Light of His Temple. And during some of these times, when I closed my eyes, I could see His Light. And there, within the Purity of His Soul, was the Priceless Pearl beyond any earthly measure. A sum much greater than the mere earth could ever hold, is the Star of Love within the Soul.

I soon heard the familiar gentle exhale of his breath as he returned from his place of comfort. **"I take pleasure"**, He said slowly, **"in the warmth of your heart. And when it speaks, I am filled with the spirit of prayer and listening. My brother, you need not answer what calls from deep within, you only need to listen. The ache of this yearning serves to get your attention. If you would know fullness, then you must learn to let go and move beyond earthly illusions, entering into the Pure Self within your Temple. The world that appears around you does not offer you peace, for only within can you find your peace; rather, the world offers separateness as experience and food for the aspiring Soul as it journeys homeward. We all are the Father's Stars of Love who now dwell beneath the veil of earthly flesh. All that life has to offer is already within you, and the doors of your Father's Kingdom, like the stars in the heavens, are Endless and divinely sustained.**

If you would know the mind, heart and the Spirit of your Father, first empty the prayer of your heart upon His altar. Then take seat within the quiet place of surrender, that you may find His Presence as the Great Shepherd of all Life. And from the cup of your love pour forth its contents, doing so in the Name of your Father, so that there within your own Temple you may find the Star and Wellspring of Love to be always full and enduring."

His words carried the ringing of bells, like the quickening of a deep remembrance, while time seemed strangely suspended. Then I heard myself ask, "I know the Father can reach from His Heavens and touch us, but You say that I may dare to reach and touch His Spirit? That is a bold thought and even now do I quake to consider it. But I have heard you say, **"What Loving Father would not desire that His Children come to sit at His table and share the sum of His good fortune with them?"** I am grateful my brother for the words that flow from Your lips. They are not of this earth and are like beacons of candlelight that rise within my soul. I shall ponder this teaching within my heart and my prayer."

"And when you do so", he added, **"Know, my brother, that the meditation of your heart is the Life Force of the Father. Liken this within yourself to a great and golden candlestick in a spiral wind that is perched with flame. See how this Light presses forth and beyond your forehead as your crown is pierced in silver-white fire. Let thy only thought be the awareness that thou art a son of God whose heart now seeks to be only in service to the Most High and have Faith that you are now welcomed at His Table and shall be fed the pure fruits and breads of your Father's Kingdom and Love.**

Let your heart be always waiting upon the Spirit of the Lord and in a quiet stillness you will hear His word within

you. Go often into your meditations with the Father and in private, not like those priests and scribes who pray only when they can be seen and heard in the presence of men. They give great outward show of their robes of holiness so that men, in error, think they walk in close union with God. They do this so that even the poor will feel they owe alms to them, thinking them to be great and godly ones and favored in the Lord's eyes. These, the poor, weak, and downtrodden, believe these priests will then intercede for them before the Lord and His mercy. Verily I tell you, James, the uncleanliness of the prayer of the greedy and unmerciful, the prideful and arrogant, is like fouled incense that rises not into the Heavens of the Most High, for it is heavy laden with the darkness and dust of the blind and deaf, and clings like a shadow to the earth. So also they shall have the reward due them, by tasting the bitterness of their own poisoned thoughts.

By the Divine Graces and Perfect Nature of the Father, We, the Sons of God, learn wisdom from our errors. Yet these poor and humble spirits who seek the mercies of God shall also be rewarded for the Father of Life is always the reader of the Heart. So has He sent me with His Word to teach and free the souls of men, in all places, in all lands, from the highest of places to the lowest and weakest among our brothers, for the Lord is not a respecter of person, but the Great and Equal Lover of all.

Let it be known that every man is the Temple of God and every Soul therefore a Portal of the Divine Nature of the Father. No doctrines carry authority, and there is no religion to be given prominence in The Kingdom of Heaven. There is no greater nor lessor to be found in the Kingdom of your Father's Heart. You need no other man or authority to give you seat before your Heavenly Father. Pray first that His Will be opened within you, for the Father brings only those gifts that are perfect and bear the nature and fruits of Divine Ripening. Be as a child who is pure and innocent, grateful for his daily bread and finding comfort at the table of his Father. Be merciful and loving in your dealings and relationships with others, for such is the Way and Spirit of your Father within you.

The Father speaks thus, "Come with me, those that are heavy laden and burdened, for Our Kingdom is not of this earthly twine. Wear the mantle of the Spirit of Love in all thy journeys so that together we bring forth Our Perfect Vision."

Chapter 25

~ My Kingdom is not of this World ~

Jeshua mystified me. When pressed by myself and others, He would deny that He was the Messiah and Leader of our people, the One prophesied to be crowned our King and savior. But then also He said to me, **"If I tell them the Truth, that I am the Messiah, the long awaited one, they will think just as you and our mother already do, that I will free our people and become a king of this land. But I shall not be as a king in this world, for my Kingdom is Not of this Earthly Domain, but of the Divine and Finer Realms of the Spirit of God Our Father. So also is this Kingdom of God that I speak of the true Kingdom of the Soul and Spirit that lives within Every Man."**

"But Jeshua," I replied, "I do not understand how You can say You are not the Messiah and yet tell me that you are the One. Therefore, according to the word of the Holy Scriptures, would you not indeed be the promised deliverer of our people?"

"I am He", he said firmly, and then paused. **"But the scriptures of our fathers are incomplete and do not contain the fullness of the Perfect Revelation of God to man. The**

sacred pages and scrolls in this world can never deliver Man into the arms of the whole of the Truth of our Heritage and the understanding of the Magnificent Nature of our Divine Creator.

If Man would be delivered from woes of all kinds, then he must be given a Light to follow. I am but the servant of the Most High and I bring the Sword of Truth and the Grace of our Father's Love. I come to all my brethren bearing fruitful seeds from the Heart of the Holy One to be planted and to flourish within the experience of man and so deliver him from the inner enslavement that afflicts so many of the earth.

We are The Sons and Daughters of Our Father's Creative Light and Companions Evermore. Behold the Spirit moves the Soul among the watery experiences of human form and mortality. These veiled and wondrous journeys are bestowed as living gifts of The Father to our Immortal and Grandest Self. But always within the Journey of Man lives the Resurrection of his Soul, for we are Above All things Temporal and are the Sons of God, made in His Eternal Image and carrying the Divine Substance of Spirit."

I shamefully resisted the Beauty and Truth of His words for I was distraught upon hearing again He would not free His people from Roman tyranny. I now passionately pressed my brother further for understanding, saying, "Does not our Father have the power and will to be merciful to our nation and remove the Roman yoke of oppression and cruelness from our backs? Hath He not heard the cries of innocents slaughtered by Herod in his search to destroy you? Does not the blood of our brothers run like a river of abomination before His eyes? Does He not see the brutal injustices that shamefully spew forth upon the hills of Golgotha? Who is this God who answers not the real needs of

His people? And why did the Lord not save John the Righteous and Great Baptizer from the sword and wrath of one so lowly and evil as the snake of Herod?"

These last words fell from my lips in sadness and desperation and I was unable to contain the accompanying tears of a breaking heart. I felt shame at resisting my most noble and pure Brother. Yet how was it, I pondered, that He still believed the spirit of my loyalty stood beside him so firmly? Had I not again bitterly questioned the Lord and His Will, doing so even here before His Messenger?

"James", said Jeshua, **"be not in dismay, for that which weighs heavily upon your heart and mind is always known and understood by the Father. Be grateful that you carry such a great spirit of justice, compassion and mercy. Let me say this of John. He is a Master Spirit and, like Elijah, this Soul is a servant of the Most High, and He shares no part of shadow and untruth for He bears no earthly fetters. The heart and center of the soul of this one is fastened quickly to The Light of Truth. John cared not about the events of his deliverance from the earth, but only that his mission would be fulfilled in the Name of the Father. But so also know that God did not will that John must be taken in the manner that occurred.**

God does not interfere with the choices men make in their earthly affairs, except in providing a pathway to the union and inspiration of His Presence, the Father's Beacon of Light found within each Temple. Know that the brutalities of man that are poured upon his brother are not the expression of the Father's Will. But All Life, in all its forms, exists and lives within the Womb of His Spirit and Love. All things created are divinely balanced, maintained and sustained by the Living Law of the Will, Structure, and

Nature of the Creative Force of Spirit. There will always be a reckoning for the darkness that Man chooses to loose upon the earth. The yokes of oppression and the bondage placed upon Israel, or any nation or people, cannot stand. That which you do to another, you have done to yourself.

Let all man pray from the deepness of their hearts that their Father's Will be their guiding Experience. Such communion opens the gates for the Kingdom of God to fully enter the Journey of Soul. The workings of the Spirit of Divine intervention may be manifested in man's experience, in accordance with the will of the Creator, when the pureness of the heart's Invitation aligns with the Father's will. God indeed does whatsoever He Wills in Perfect Infinite Wisdom and Love without Measure for his children.

There is a door to His Spirit that opens when a man or woman chooses love and compassion, mercy and forgiveness as the living mantle and breastplate of his earthly walk. These attributes of the Spirit and Soul find their physical embodiment throughout the material universe."

And though my soul was confused and full of anguish, I knew He would answer my plea for peace and deliverance from my unrest. The welcomed touch of His hand and the grip of His arms was not of this world for it transported and delivered me into a Peace that was greater than my mind could comprehend. A river of deep knowing and healing flowed gently into my ears, like music drifting from Paradise, and the oil and flame of His deep and abiding love and kindness brought my soul to its knees.

And from there did I see the Pasture of the Son of God within me and within all, and it was Good Beyond any measure, and I sang praise for I was humbled and uplifted before the Light of the Maker. I would give honor to my Father's Life within me and follow Him all the days of my life. I knew but one prayer of Truth within me. "Let me be only the Heart and Hands of Thee my Lord of Divine Truth and Light." And I give thanks for this vision: We are all Eternally found to be within the Presence and True Brilliance of the Holy One.

Chapter 26

~ After the time of my Mission being Complete ~

One day, upon the hills of Judah, while taking a short time away from His apostles, disciples and followers, Jeshua sat with Jude and I and spoke of the future, and of many marvelous revelations regarding the universe of God, saying, **"After the time of my mission being complete, the message of my teaching will not remain in the same purity as I have given it to you. Some will speak of me as one who should be worshiped and they will build great temples in my name. These things I have seen and they will manifest in the world for an age. But when they put me upon a pedestal they distance themselves in understanding. They will make me to be of such divine personage that they see themselves to be of lesser value and stature than the Father. That is a great untruth. All souls are the Sons and Daughters and Companions of Our Father, the Holy and the Unending One. We have journeyed far upon the bosom of His Wondrous Presence and through eons of time, though the true realm of the soul is timeless.**

We experience ourselves in many forms. Behold how glorious is the human form, though greater still are there forms of divine and wondrous construction within the planes of the spiritual and also those physical, and they are without number. It is the will of the Lord that the soul may choose to live the life of man, to pass beneath the Veil of Separateness and net the earthly experiences it desires. But it is the Law of His Grace and Love that All life is bound and bathed in the River of the One True Light. And when you are without this body, you know yourself to be this River and Blessed within the Waters of the Eternal.

Man, within the consciousness of his soul, is accountable for what he creates. So what he does to another he has done to all and to himself. To forgive another is to unchain ourselves from this bondage, thus making more room for the Spirit of Love to enter our heart. Do no harm, for it returns to you tomorrow; forgive others, and yourself, and know that your transgressions from the past are always dissolved in the Grace and Loving Spirit of God.

Chapter 27

~The Crippled Child~

Jeshua ministered to all in His Path. To the crying child whose legs were bowed and ankles twisted, wrapped in his young mother's arms as she laid him upon His lap. She shook and trembled with emotion, pleading in grief and desperation for her son to be straightened and well. Jeshua's apostles and all present were moved with sadness and compassion. They looked hopefully at Jeshua, who cradled the writhing child upon His legs and knees, and smiled tenderly, saying, **" So shall this be done."** He said to Jude, **"Bring me the cup of oil."** He took the oil of olives, dipped His fingers and applied the moisture to the legs and feet. Jeshua then placed His hands at the top of each leg, gently massaging the limbs over, under, and slowly downward, and the limbs seemingly melted into a normal shape. The mother gasped and was breathless and fell to her knees in tears of shock and happiness, and Jeshua gently pulled the child's small ankles and they became straight upon the feet, and the child smiled and giggled with delight and we all wept with joy and astonishment and thanked the Lord for this miracle of Divine Love, Grace and Mercy. Jeshua then lifted the child onto his feet, holding his little hands as the child steadied himself? For a moment he looked confused, but then squealed excitedly in an exploding smile as his feet pounded the ground with glee. I was not present for many of Jeshua's healing miracles, but nothing moved me more than the transformation of this child's mother. She clung to Jeshua, her arms around His neck and her tears dropping onto His cheek as she whispered "Thank you, my Lord, Oh sweet Rabbi, thank you."

Jeshua smiled and handed her child into her arms saying, **"Go now in peace my young sister, and know that this soul shall grow strong and tall, and walk a straight and sturdy path upon the earth, sharing the burdens of the lame and crippled in body and spirit, bringing Hope and Comfort to many, all in the name and service of Our Heavenly Father."**

Chapter 28

~The Kingdom of The Father~

John said with a passionate, humble, and deep sincerity, "Tell us, Jeshua, of the land of our Father. What can you say to us that we may partake of His Glorious Mansions, now, while we walk upon this earth? Could we come to see and know the fullness of His Spirit within us, as fully as He resides within you?" **"My Brothers"**, Jeshua began slowly, **"You ask the question I have been sent to answer. The Kingdom you seek is within you. Each one must ask themselves, "For what reason do I seek to know of my Creator?" Some might think that knowing of the Father brings stature over other men, and it may, but that does not make a deliverer of peace. You may believe it pleases the Father that you would seek reunion with His Spirit, and it does when it springs from a deep stirring and longing within your Heart. Look then to awaken the innocence of the child within you for it is the child that wishes no one harm and trusts their mother and their father to care for them, the child who delights in the rising of the sun and the birds announcing "let it begin again", the child who knows laughter in the wind and that amazement will** surely fill the new day. And it is right to know joy, so remember to dwell upon these things now. Take thyself into a quiet place, be it a bed, or beside a stream that soothes the mind and quiets the body, or walk among the field of olive branches or wheat, or find an altar that opens its doors to your kind and gentle knocking. Speak your heart unto your Father, call for His will to be perfect, blessed and free to move through you. Know that You are the Flute of His Thoughts of Love. For the Father sees only the Beauty and Eternal Goodness of Creation and Sustains it in Divine Meadows of All Light and Brilliance, where there is No Time, for All time, is already Here. You are a Gift to God, and a gift unto yourself. You are the child and son of Blessed Intention, a Star cast upon All the Heavens and Its infinite Meadows of Joy and Peace. Go then into your prayer and float upon the stream of the Goodness that flows within you, and become still, in the knowing that you have thus placed your heart into the Heart of God, and have then faith that you have now become the Sun of His Will, which is Love. And for a moment of each hour, give thanks and remembrance for your Union within Him."

A deep and gentle wave of silence filled the air between each Man and his Soul. Jeshua had opened a door before us, beckoning for us to earnestly seek the Light and Life of the Father Within. He wanted us to **"Know thyself to be the Precious and Eternal Child of the Master Spirit of the Heavens and Earth. Walk deeply into the Heart of Love and its Waters, where you will find Peace and Strength, Grace and Mercy and you shall you find your needs are filled and your thirst quenched. You will find Gratefulness has Wings that lift you higher into The Arms of the Holy One. Then rest upon His Breast, pray that goodness, health, and comfort be blessed upon your friends** and neighbors, your family, and Every-man that is in need and hungers for Peace. Pray then for those who know not of the Table of The Lord that is set before them, that they also would find the stillness of a gentle Light that burns within them, and come to know the deep warmth that carries their heart and soul thru all Eternity. Lay then your ear before the Voice, that says always, I and my Father, are One."

He wanted us to seek and find our connection to Our Father, and one another. Jeshua knew we all would need to find the spirit of courage and faith within us, for we would soon be without Him. "**You will look for me, and find me not in the flesh, for I will be taken from its form. And each of you will be in turmoil and fear, but I shall not forsake you. I shall rise from within this body and after three days I will come and see and speak to you my true brothers, and you shall know joy and peace on that morning. And I will ascend unto the realm of Our Father with His task accomplished which is to have demonstrated before all Man that the Father Lives, that Love is the Bread of His Spirit and always within you, and that you can never be banished from the Meadows of His Infinite Heart, for you are His Beloved Son, Daughter, and Companion, Evermore. And the Father will send a Great Breath of Holiness into your hearts and minds that will carry and lead you on your path, while loving others as I have loved you. I tell you these things now, so in that time you will come to more fully believe in me and Our Father who has sent me.**"

We were spellbound, for He was telling each of us that He would be leaving this world. The sadness took my breath away, though I knew that was not His intention, His eyes grew deep with compassion, for He knew that for his disciples there was no peace in this Truth but rather consternation and confusion. What future event would take Our Master from our side?

Chapter 29

~Our Father's Purposes and Will~

Jeshua said, "The Lord your Father has given us Eternal life. We are given a perfect and vast gift of Divine Substance, for we are to be the carriers of His Heart, thru the Rivers of His Light, among the mansions of Realms Spiritual and Planes Unnumbered, and to spread the Light of Love created into the unfolding Paradise of a Perfect Unity, always and forever.

These things are truth spoken, though not easily understood, yet each of you shall find your living treasure within you. A divine and holy Spark as tiny as a grain of sand, yet this True Self encompasses the Breath of Creation. Verily I tell thee, thou art the Blessed Sons and Daughters of a Holy One.

Chapter 30

~The Gift of a Woman~

I spoke unto my Brother: " You have said to me that you shall not marry in this life, and it troubles and saddens me that it is so for one who is so deeply instilled in the Spirit of Love. Is there no room for the tenderness of a woman's company, a companion loyal and comforting, and beside you always?" Thus, with a sparkle in His eyes, and a soft smile, did He reply, **"The Gift of a Woman is a Blessed Union, and I have known its wonder in lifetimes times before. I recall the pleasures of the heart and body, laughter and gaiety, the birth of innocent babes, nurturing their sons and their daughters in a strong and tender love; the comfort of a smile and a gentle whisper of love in my ear. Yes, I remember well.**

I am grateful to have known love's valleys and its peaks. So has my Soul journeyed thru the many paths of Man so I might better serve my Fathers purposes by understanding the separation of the Soul from the Remembrance of its true heavenly abode and Heritage, that being the Glory of His Spiritual Pastures of Love and Eternal Life.

Thus have I been prepared to bring His Heart and Will before the eyes and ears of those, His children of Divine Issue, who have strayed into a darkness of forgetfulness and know not of what they do and what they shall reap.

I come to serve His Will, fully and without pause or hesitation, in accordance with His Word alive within me.

His Love is undivided and equally bestowed upon all. There is a season for all the things of Heaven and Earth, and this is the Season of the Resurrection of Truth and Light before the Sons and Daughters of The Holy One, to Whom my Heart, Soul, Mind and Body is given in complete marriage and attunement."

It was an exquisite answer, but my humanly fostered sadness remained drifting thru my heart, for he was my Brother, first and always, and I would forever want his path to be safe, without peril, and peace laden. I knew that I would not be able to change my deepest concerns and wishes for his wellbeing, and I was caught in a quicksand of futile hopes over things I could not and would never control.

Chapter 31

~The Olive Fields~

One day Jeshua bade that I come walk with Him in the olive fields. The skies were blue with billowing white clouds. There was a warm breeze and birds sang and danced among the branches and seemed to welcome us to their sanctuary. **"James"**, He said, **"It is time for me to prepare you for the coming trials that soon shall envelop our lives, our purposes and our earthly missions."** He stopped and turned to me, placing His right hand upon my heart and His left hand upon my right shoulder. He began slowly: **"Fear not this moment of Truth, for mercy fills this moment though I know you tremble with uncertainty. In this very place I will come beside you soon after the resurrection of this, my temple of flesh. I will come quickly to end your pain and confusion. I will restore your spirit and faith in me and He who hath sent me into the world. For you will drown in human doubt and trepidation for what shall befall me upon a cross. I will fulfill my task and, in my resurrection, complete my mission to show all those within the earth for all ages to come, the Truth of the Eternal Soul and Life Hereafter."**

I looked away from Him, my teeth clenched. My body shook with anger, frustration and fear. "No I cried. No, tell me not of such things that crush my heart and bleed life and hope from my days. For what crime shall they take you from us? For healing the sick and the blind? Feeding the poor and hungry? Giving wise and tender council to the downhearted and hopeless? Why would your kindness bring such injustice?" **"James"**, he said softly. **"Kindness and love do not breed injustice. Rather shall it undue the origins of such darkness in the lives of man. We are betrayed by the blindness that grips those who would harm me. They see only their own thrones as being their seat of happiness and well being and they turn their back on the True God of Love, Mercy and Grace. And I forgive them. The Father within forgives even before repentance, for He knows His Children have strayed into dark waters, illusions, and untruth. So hath He sent a Light into this world to point the Way Home.**

Injustice and cruelty are illnesses of the mind that dampen the light within the heart and wreak turmoil in the lives of men.

Man, in his fall from the Heavenly Realms where Truth, Light and Love are the Eternal Reality, often finds himself caught up in his human impulses, so that his choices are weighed down in fear, confusion, and ungodliness. And from such entanglement he must be set free, for he knows not what he does, nor of his True and Holy self.

The powerful of the earth who misuse their places of authority over man create discord and resentment in the minds of their people. They sow seeds of discontent by their greed, unfairness and lack of compassion for the poor and weak of body and the hopeless of spirit. They subjugate their brothers and sisters and cling to their own riches,

comforts and stature. But these are hollow and bring them no peace until they awaken to the Light within them and seek to raise up the spirits of every man, and share with them their comforts and recognize the equality of the True Brotherhood of Man and his Soul within the Father's Many Mansions." "But Jeshua," I replied. "Why cannot God shed His Light upon these men now and bring their hearts into the pastures of love and understanding, and change these men who sow misery and contempt for others?" **"James"**, He said, **"He gave the soul, and therefore Man, free will. A Gift to all for all time. For His Light and Perfect Love is never diminished. His Patience and Grace are without measure, and will follow you in all your choices and paths. All His children are destined for the Glory of His Kingdoms. They will learn from their errors, meet what they have sown, and over the ages return to their Father's pastures. Henceforth will they praise Him in wonderment and gratefulness for the Table of the Father which lays before and Within them always."

Chapter 32

~The Fields of Forgiveness~

Jeshua said, "When a man falls and fails himself on this earthly path, lo, will he hear the whisper of his spirit from within his soul. So must he understand the Fields of Forgiveness. Soon then should he repent and seek to be clean. And as above, so also below comes a Holy Reflection of the Father's Love for His Children. Therefore turn your heart and mind to face the Light of your Father, where you are invited into His Fields of Grace and Peace. Release then your grip on the weeds of guilt and shame, that the pure fullness of your soul may be freed of its weight. For you do not honor your God nor your brethren by pulling a cover of heavy darkness over the Light of your Soul. Rather bathe in His Delight that you have returned to the Pure Paradise of loving service to His ways of grace, compassion, mercy and understanding.

Behold there is a stream of Light that beckons you home, where your finest self is Forever your Greatest Treasure. Tarry not among the weeds of those thoughts that would condemn thyself. Rather be he that would bring peace to others, and you will find your peace. What you give to another, so do you receive that same gift from within thyself.

I look about this world and its troubles, and I know there are seasons for all things. But I see through the Eyes of my Father who Knows you to be Clean by the very Spark of Life He planted deeply and forever within you. Seek always to walk upon the meadows of His Golden Heart that keeps you close in its warmth, and feel its strength, gentleness, and sureness of support.

Forgiveness in all its forms, for yourself and others, shall spread like a tree with many branches and bring its peace to this world. One day so shall it be, that the lion shall lie down with the lamb and they will be warm together. Behold how the sheep has no fear and the lion hungers not."

Chapter 33

~The Sorrows of Man~

"Jeshua," I asked. "Why do sorrows and suffering afflict our people and those of many nations, near and far? Is there no peace among men to be found anywhere in this world?"

"Sadly", He said, **"there is no village or nation that has not seen conflict. And sorrowful times arise within every man's life. The Soul yearns for peace and brotherhood to be found within it and to find harmony with all that lies within our Father's Many Mansions. But each soul creates his journey and so he swims in these dreams, be they bright or thickly dark. Our choices are given to us that we may see and know of their worth and place within the Pure Watchfulness of the Father's Heart. And from our suffering, so also comes our longing for peace.**

God has willed that none shall perish from His Hands. You carry the True Spark of His Light that cannot escape His Truth and His Beauty, though the soul's journey descends to earthly forms, where it knows not of His Heavenly Birthplace, and easily falls into traps and trepidation. Many fears confront Man in this cloak of

darkness, and his suffering is increased in its depth and despair.

But Our Father is mindful of our difficulties, for He is a listener of The Heart. And I have come to bring His Light, His Truth, and the Way Home for my Brothers and Sisters who long for His Will to be brightly spilled into the shadows of their Days and Nights. And His Way is Love, Peace, Forgiveness and the Nurturing of Kindness and Compassion. Therefore, Judge Not, that you may not find judgment against you, on your path.

Behold the blind man who suffers even from birth and knows not peace unless he is lifted up on the arms of another who would lead him to water and comfort. See how the lame suffer in pain until given a staff and the sturdiness of an arm about their waist. See how one can, through Love, bring forth a gift of healing into their life and ease their calamities. Be the bearer of Goodness to another, as you would have done unto you. These are the steps to bring man out of the depths of suffering and contention, and all man must learn mercy and forgiveness that this world may be restored to the Vision and Remembrance of a Paradise that shines within Us."

Chapter 34

~The Heart, So Saith Jeshua~

"The Heart is the doorway to your Holy Self. And he that finds and knows its treasures shall see his God and Father within him.

It is the Giver of Life, and its fields widen and open to the pureness of a yearning within you to Feel and Be Home Again and Whole.

Your heart knows the pathway to your Father, for He hath set Himself there, in closeness to His Beloved Children and Companions Evermore. In thy prayer, knock upon the door to His Spirit and it Shall be Opened. Let thy first knock be filled with Thankfulness, for Love then takes wings, and the Light brightens beyond the door's edges, for your Father is pleased in your homecoming and would fill His Table with fruits and breads, wines and figs, and lay them before you. And with thy second knock offer him the Cup of your Heart, that it might be filled with his Will and Love, to be passed to all who would be found along your paths and journeys.

And on thy third knocking, love Him with thy whole heart, mind, soul, and body, as a Son or Daughter loves the Presence of their Father-Mother. From Whom you were born, carry the Divinity of His Seed thru Eternity and Beyond. And know then now, in this world, He may be known. His Life force breathes thru the vessels of your beating Heart. Let thy river flow with Streams of Kindness and Love, encircling all brothers and sisters great and small. The Gift of your Soul is a Priceless Pearl, for it bears the Flame of Brilliance and Breath of Pure Light and Life.

Be then the Seeker of His Face within you. Let the Meditation of your Heart be your guide, and you will Hear His Word and See your Name written in the Book of His Heart where there is no shadow to be found. Though in this world there are many shadows of untruth, know that these forms cannot endure in the Light of His Will and Love, and so will come Peace within the Soul, and Goodwill to all men.

Behold you carry the Ark of the Covenant within your Heart, adorned with the jewels of a golden love and silver grace. See how the diamonds of mercy and understanding may be found here already set within this your Temple of The Son of God."

Chapter 35

~ After the Last Supper ~

I followed Jeshua and His apostles out the door and into the street beneath the starlit night. He drew me aside, softly but urgently saying, **"James, my dearest brother, you must go now. My time has come and I need you to care for our family. Do not follow me, nor where I go nor where I am taken. Stay with your brothers and sisters no matter what news reaches your ears. Our mother will not be so easily persuaded to keep a distance, and so shall it be. But it is best for you to keep our family safe and I will see you again, I promise."** He took my hands, kissed my cheek, looked me in the eyes and said, **"Go now"**, and turned away to join the others. My body seemed frozen as I watched Him drift among the group and then I saw Him look from the corner of His eye at me, and I felt a jolt up my spine and suddenly my legs began their journey home but my heart was not in agreement with my steps.

Word came quickly that morning from Andrew of His arrest. Betrayed by Judas, who brought a band of Jewish Temple Soldiers and Roman guards to Gethsemane. My mind was crushed in a whirlpool of despair, a quicksand of darkness, and then a perilous pit of caged anger. Love abandoned my heart. The seditious scorn of simple kindness and compassion that these self-flattering and greedy Sanhedrin possessed, made me fully their enemy. How dare they take this precious Lamb of Godly Light and bind Him like a criminal? In my mind, I plunged my sword deeply into their already deadened hearts. Only then did I weep, hard... and long.

My mother, accompanied by my brother Jude, left for Jerusalem. I would care for my other siblings. That night, my sister Ruth awakened and came to me with trembling voice, saying "James, I dreamed that I was floating above Jeshua, who was on a cross, and He looked up at me and said, **"Fear not my sweet sister, I will always be with you"**, but James, I am afraid... very afraid," she said in quiet desperation. I pulled her into my arms, as I gasped for air. That was the moment that I knew fully that His vision was true, that **"upon a cross, He would expire"**; a vision I had so wanted to have been wrong. I led her back to her bed, handed her the small wooden boat that Jeshua had carved for her, and sat beside her till she slept.

My mother returned with Jude two days later. I saw her approaching, leaning on Jude's arm. She was a mother broken, her eyes red and swollen, her face gray, and her legs stumbling and without strength. I could not bear the sight of her suffering as she looked up at me. She fell forward into my shaking arms, with a heavy moan, able only to whisper my name.

"Oh Mother," was all that escaped my lips. Whereupon I lifted her like a child, cradled in my arms, my tears silently falling upon her face, and I carried her into our home. I stood holding her for a time for I could not let her go from my gently clutching arms. Only then did she cry out in agony, **"They have taken... my Son,... my lamb,... my Jeshua."**

The sound of those words echoed like thunder through my being, and I would never forget nor stop hearing them for the rest of my life, and the life hereafter.

Chapter 36

~Jeshua Appears to me Among The Olive Trees~

It was the third day after Jeshua's death. My family and I were deep in grief and despair. I was fully and sadly consumed with doubt that He would or could rise from the tomb as He had told me and His closest disciples He would. But I knew I must go to the olive fields as He had previously instructed me to do. With what little strength I possessed, and with less than a whisper of any hope, I pushed myself, one step at a time, towards that destination. I felt foolish and disheartened as I proceeded onward, with less "**faith than a grain of mustard seed**", and I, in the midst of all my inner turbulence, was also ashamed, for it seemed that once again, I had let go of His Hand.

Nevertheless, in under an hour, I saw the grove of olive trees before me. The sky was filled with billowing white clouds, which had provided shade from the hot sun this morning. But as I approached, the clouds began to separate, and deep blue sky appeared between them, and the sun lit the grove of olives before me.

I ventured into their midst as the birds darted among them, singing cheerfully in a winged dance that comforted my troubled soul. I found the set of trees that I remembered Jeshua and I had talked beside and I rested there to catch my breath. After a moment, I cupped my hands over my face, eyes, and mouth, and prayed simply, "My Father, my God, have mercy on my family, and the soul of Jeshua. And as my earthly father taught me to pray, may Thy Will be done".

Suddenly the air became hushed and quiet, and the birds were silent, and from behind me came His voice, **"James, Let not your heart be troubled further. Neither be ye afraid, for I am here."**

My hands fell from my face, my body stiffened. I turned, and there before me was a bluish mist like sparkling diamonds in the shape of a man, and just as suddenly it then became Jeshua! I burst into tears; my body trembled like never before as shock and Joy beyond understanding rolled thru me like thunder, as all my despair fled my being as if never there and I exclaimed, "You Live, Jeshua, You Live. My God, You Live!" I dropped to my knees in joyous weeping and all the darkness that had consumed me was gone in an instant! "Forgive me, my Father, my God, my Brother, I am Healed, Humbled and Blessed beyond all Measure!" **"Peace be with you my good brother. Arise, For I would speak with thee and shortly I must visit our family and bring Peace also to their heavy hearts, minds and souls. Glory be to the Father for His Love and Power is now proclaimed throughout His Heavens and His Earth, and for all the Ages, now, and to come. I will also go before my closest disciples and heal their fears, and ready them for the Gift of the Father's Holy Spirit to move upon and within them to carry the Truth of our Heavenly Creator to the ends of the earth and for all time. And before I ascend to the**

Throne of My Father, I will visit many lands and peoples, for, being His Shepherd, I must bring them also into the fold of His flock.

James, care for your family as you have done, and be ye good council to my apostles should they need help and direction, doing such in my name. And to you I do promise that in the hour of your resurrection from your body, I will come beside you, and you will see me in my body of Holy Fire and I will take your hand and lead you into the Paradise of Our Father's Heart and Spirit, where we will sup together at His Holy Table.

Then, in another Age upon this earth, I will return to lead our brothers and sisters into an Age of Peace and Enlightenment, and many of you will I ask to go forth with me, in service to the Father's Will. But now, My Peace be with you. And know, I will always be with you. Glory Be Unto Our Father." And then He was gone.

With new found strength and joy in my step, I began my journey home. When I was in sight of my home, I saw my family standing before it, my siblings surrounding my mother. And when they saw me, my sister Ruth broke from the group and ran towards me, crying, "He Lives, James, He Lives!" Into my arms she ran and I squeezed her joyfully, saying, "Indeed, Indeed He Lives!"

Chapter 37

~ Shalom said the Roman Visitor~

It had been about three months since Jeshua's crucifixion and Resurrection. **"James"**, said my mother. **"Awaken, for a man approaches."**

I hurriedly arose from my bedding, rubbing sleep from my eyes. I stepped into the doorway where I beheld a tall man walking with his horse in hand. The sun was just rising behind him and his form shimmered in the dust of his approach. "Mother, go inside for I know not who this man might be." He walked slowly and seemed not menacing, but I was puzzled for I could not recognize him nor the horse he led. I called out to him, "Who art thou and what business have you here?" "Shalom, Shalom," he said with a deep voice that seemed to carry a nervousness in its delivery. He stopped and begged that he might approach and offered that he meant no harm. I nodded and waved for him to proceed. As he came closer I could see his face had only the beginnings of a dark beard and his features were perhaps more gentile than Hebrew. I was somewhat alarmed as I wondered if he could be Roman in Jewish garb.

He suddenly stopped and fell to his knees and his body shook. His head lowered and tears burst from his eyes as he exclaimed, "I am not worthy to come closer. though I am Roman I pledge my allegiance to your Hebrew God and seek your forgiveness." But he could speak no more for his grief consumed him. He fell forward in cries of agony. My legs were weak with astonishment as I approached him slowly. "What is your name, brother?" He could not immediately speak, but when his breath returned, he whispered, "Marcus."

At last, he pushed himself back up onto his knees. He then cried out, "I am a grievous sinner of the lowest form and I shall not remain long in your presence. I want only to confess my sin against you, your family, your people and your God, and then I shall withdraw this day from these lands and peoples."

"Marcus," I said softly, "was it by your hand that my brother Jeshua was crucified?" He shook his head and clenched his hands to his chest, and said between his gritted teeth, "I scourged Him, an innocent lamb. I scourged Him, being unable to be merciful. For I was a soldier and took honor in following orders. But no more. There is no honor nor justice in the brutal punishing of any man. Each lashing drew sobs of regret and tears from my heart and now I wish these guilty hands severed from my limbs, that they may sin no more. My commanders laughed at me as I wept during this flogging. I wished that I could stop and let them drive a spear thru my heart, but I was weak and I obeyed their merciless demands."

I turned to see my mother in the doorway, and tears fell like rain upon her face. I cried, "Mother, no please...", but she silently clasped her hands to her lips and motioned *NO* with her head as she stepped thru the door and stood beside me. "Oh thou blessed woman," Marcus began, "Though I am not worthy to look upon you, I must tell you of the greatest of all miracles that your Son brought before my eyes and heart. In the week following His death, I swear did He come upon me while I lay in grief upon my cot wanting to live no more. He said only the words, **"I have forgiven thee, and My Father as well forgives you. Lay down your whips, leave this land, and love and protect others"** and He vanished before my eyes!

My mother stepped before Marcus and gently inquired, **"How is it you knew of my Son's innocence?"** Marcus replied, "Many months ago, I was sent to spy on Jeshua by Pilate, to see if he posed a threat to his reign over the Hebrews. I heard Jeshua speak. His words were Godly, Peace filled, Kind and Compassionate to All people, and wisdom fell from His lips, like no other I had ever heard. And I reported to my superiors that this man is a holy and good man who offers No threat to us."

My mother stepped forward and placed her hands around his, beckoning him to rise. He did so with a bowed head and her tears fell upon his hands, whereupon she kissed them gently and said unto Marcus, " **So has my Son forgiven you, and in His honor so also do I. May you go forth in Peace, and do as He commanded. Love and protect the innocent on your journey for you are now of His fold, always**." Marcus replied, "And so it shall be, blessed woman. I will seek to join caravans traveling to the East where I may find new life and purpose." "Marcus," I said, "do you require water or bread?" "No," he replied. "As you see, my horse is well laden for the journey. I shall never forget your kindness and mercy. Peace be with your family always." "Marcus," I assured him, "we shall never tell anyone of your visit, that you may be safe from Roman pursuers."

He nodded gratefully, turned and went on his way. I put my arm around my mother, and together we watched him slowly disappear into the rising sun.

Chapter 38

~Be Not Afraid, It is I.

Resurrection-A Golden Sunset~

I was summoned by a dubiously selected handful of Sanhedrin to give answer to the criticisms of blasphemy as held in the minds of these certain Judges and Keepers of the Law. I knew always of their thoughts. That I knew them even better than they knew themselves, made me, sadly, a threat. As well did they hold me in great disdain, for I was beloved by many people and widely respected for the love and wisdom that I shared freely among those who searched for justice or healing in their life. To each one, I endeavored to show the simple tools of fairness and respect, kindness and mercy.

On this early evening, the halls were eerily cold and thickly filled with the venomous spirits and shadows of jackals, the blind and deaf of the pompous scribes and Pharisees and Sadducees. Their eyes turned upon me as I took the steps upward to the Room of the Altar.

Then I began my prayer and resurrection, saying, "I am humbled by Your Grace my Father and blessed to have walked with my brother Jeshua, the Divine Messenger of Love from the Heart and Core of the Most High Realm of Thy Spirit. My Father, at last I climb these hills, and I see the Path of Your Hand is beneath my feet and though a dark cloud would surround me, it touches me not for I am here in the Light of You my Lord. I see before me Thou hast suspended a golden sunset upon the hill that awaits the resurrection of my soul into the Greater Arms of Truth and behold how it brightens with my every step."

The monotone voice of one already decided on the certainty of my guilt and the course to be soon taken, spoke loudly, "We implore you, James, that you should bring peace and not division to our people, so that by your own testimony you may be judged. Speak, and stand upon the steps of the altar, so that all the people below you who have gathered on the streets, may hear you. What say you of your brother Jeshua? Would you proclaim before the God of Israel that he was the Messiah, the Christ and the Promised One?"

I turned on the steps to face the window. And there stood Jeshua in the glorified Light of Holy-Fire, saying, **"James, leave with them the Truth, and follow me."** And then, as if from a part distant from me, I heard myself saying, **"Yes, my Brother was the Promised One, the Messiah spoken of by the Prophets of Elohim, and He came and walked among us so that every man could know of the Divine Truth within his Temple, where resides the Eternal Light of the Father. And the Father so loves His Children that He sent His Way-Shower into this world. Jeshua was the Star of Love, the Christed One and Holy Anointed by God the Father and you knew Him not. Even now He sits at the Table of our Father God, and rejoice for there will come a time when His Light shall be seen again in the Heavens, and on a great cloud of**

Divine Construction, He shall come upon the earth, to be seen and heard and walk again among us as His Brethren.

Even now do I see Him before me, and He beckons that I should now follow Him beyond this world and into the Meadows of Paradise, as laid forth by the Hand and Heart of The Lord my God."

And a voice in bitter rage growled, "Take him now and cast him down upon the steps, and even to the ground below, that the people shall greatly fear our judgment and not believe his blasphemous words to have merit."

The steps were of hard stone and I heard the sound of deep snaps to the bones of my body, and then came a blinding light as my head came to a sudden rest on the marble floor. I saw my body rushed to the window and hurled down, but it seemed I was not truly in it. "Stone him," another voice cried, "even into the bowels of the earth, so that we might never hear again of this Jeshua, that some called the King of the Jews and the Son of God."

"James", Jeshua whispered close to my ear, **"Be not afraid, I am here."** "My Lord," I exclaimed, "I rejoice, for I forgive those that harm me, and I near the True and Eternal perfect place of my soul."

"Cease the stoning of this just and upright man who even now speaks of your forgiveness before the Lord God," cried a man's voice in a painful and desperate plea of remorse, but I was at peace.

"Into the Hands and Author of my Spirit, do I commend my Soul." A final blow was then laid upon my head and I was free to follow the Light of the Great One.

I weep in great relief as I feel the warm waters of home. A soul deep fountain of gratefulness sobs forth from within

me. Finally, I am again in the Place of My True Self. Peace fills and spills its Exquisite Light through all the space of my being. My boundaries widen as I swell with joy beyond measure. I am submerged in my Father's Light, as are so many here. I am my Father's Light and He takes Perfect Pleasure in me. In a Rushing Fountain of Perfect Love, I am drowned in ecstasy here in the Sweetness of the Mansion of my Father, which I have never left. And I see each of you to also be here, for together we are the Living Spirit of Divine Truth, begotten of The First Source, The Father of Lights, the Mother of Eternal Glory and Love without Measure.

The End,
truly which can never be.

About the Author

I was born in the Midwest, U.S.A in the early 1950's. Raised among 8 brothers and sisters, with a Catholic upbringing.

In the early 1970's I was blessed with several very personal spiritual experiences that briefly took me beyond this world, exposing me to understand the factual reality of the existence of a Heavenly Creator and our Eternal Soul. I don't walk on water and wish to remain quietly anonymous. In 1985 I moved to the mountains and lakes of Great Northwest, USA, where I gratefully reside to this day. I wish you peace, and wellness.

Sincerely,
James Francis.

Acknowledgements

My deepest thanks and appreciation to my longest friends, Peggy and Farley, for your priceless support made this work possible.

Love,
James

www.ingramcontent.com/pod-product-compliance
Lightning Source LLC
Chambersburg PA
CBHW031545080526
44588CB00018B/2710